Shoebox Full of Toads
Farewell to Mom

Tim Ghianni

PUBLISHED BY WESTVIEW, INC.
KINGSTON SPRINGS, TN 37082

PUBLISHED BY WESTVIEW, INC.
P.O. Box 605
Kingston Springs, TN 37082
www.publishedbywestview.com

ISBN 978-1-62880-008-1

First edition, October 2013

All photos from Tim Ghianni's personal collection.

Dedicated to Mom

and to all mothers, living and dead

Table of Contents

"I saw the light" 1
Silent hope... 3
Not even Sinatra helped this time 8
'She's going now' 12
She wore her pink suit.. 16
The shooting star and the bird 19
She finally saw the light 21
Love just came spilling out.. 24
'Remember me when you get to the Pacific Ocean' 26
We had our heads shaved 30
Chickens with their heads cut off.. 32
'I bit him back'... 34
'Just good old Americans'... 35
Let the music play.. 41
Birmingham and The Stones 43
Easing the pain in our hearts... 45
The best mom a kid could have.. 55
A little dance at the world premiere.. 62
Ol' Buddy, Ol' Pal 64
More fried than frazzled... 68
An ending worthy of Frank Capra 76
Confronting mortality 78
'We are the Dingbats' 81
A shoebox full of toads.. 89
Beautiful smell of fried perch.. 92
Walnut Lake... 97
Don't go away 99
Revisiting Flapjacks... 102
'Will The Circle Be Unbroken?' 106
Kiss her goodbye... 108
Remember when...? 110
Some things I wanted to say 113
No more 116
A spot on the ceiling... 117
See you later 119

Preface

It has been said that right before you die, your whole life passes before your eyes.

In my case, my whole life passed before my eyes right before my mom died.

I was there as she began the passage from this life to the next.

For a long time, I had thought about what I would want to say to Mom before she died, but now I was faced with that reality. It was time to say all those things...time to recall all those things that shaped our lives. But now would I have time to get it out? Sometimes random, often rambling...

...the final hours with Mom.

CHAPTER ONE

"I saw the light"

"Hi Mom, it's Tim."

It's the way I'd start so many of my one-sided conversations with this woman in recent days.

I stroked her pure white widow's peak and looked at her closed eyes.

"It's okay to stop fighting now, Mom. We'll be okay. We'll miss you. But you've done your job. It's okay."

I rubbed her hand.

"It's really okay." Maybe I heard a sigh. Or maybe it was just my own.

After years of struggles with Alpha-1 Antitrypsin deficiency, a genetic lung disorder, my mom was on her deathbed in the Critical Care Unit.

She'd been there for seven days by the time I said those words.

I'd been spoiled.

She'd been on the brink of death before. And she had always bounced back...worse for wear, sure, but still there, ready to fight another day. I'd never told her it was all right to do otherwise. I always tearfully stayed by her bed and told her I needed her alive. I wasn't ready to say goodbye to my mom yet. Until that night.

"It's okay to die, Mom."

The morning after I told Mom it was okay, my dad went to get coffee to fuel his bedside vigil by this beautiful woman — yes, mothers always are beautiful even when bruised by too many needles and procedures on frail skin, even when emaciated by mortal disease. Shuffling back into the CCU room, he was stopped in his tracks.

The sunrise filled the room, encircling Mom's face.

Dad told me about it a few minutes later, after I stumbled from my semi-sleep in an empty hospital room down the hall.

If a nurse hadn't seen the whole thing, backing up Dad's story of the sun providing a halo, I'd have thought he was hallucinating from lack of sleep.

These had been nights when we killed pot after pot of coffee from the hospital cafeteria. Heavily sugared and caffeinated, we hoped to be awake long enough to see her stir.

Or clutch her when she died.

After the angelic glow of the sunrise on her face, Dad stood by his war bride, his wife of 54 years and read the 23rd Psalm, something she recited each night as her health continued to spiral downward.

Yea, though I walk through the valley of the shadow of death...That shadow had been cast on the linoleum floor of the CCU by the bright, white sunrise. Peace shone on her face.

"It was her soul leaving her," Dad told me, later, as we looked down on the barely-clinging-to-life woman.

"I saw the light."

CHAPTER TWO

Silent hope

She saw the light, too.

It was a similar light that my mother had seen a few months earlier, when I got a call at work that she had gone.

"We've lost Mother," my dad said, in a hasty phone call from the hospital as doctors worked on her.

A few moments later, my brother, Eric, called to say: "Mom's in a coma. You'd better get down here to the hospital. But don't have a wreck."

Tears welled up as I told my boss I had to leave and why. It was one of those times when you try to be brave.

"I'll get my guys organized; send them notes about things that have to be done."

My boss shooed me out the door. Course, as a detail-oriented entertainment editor at the local newspaper, I had left notes enough for my guys. It was a few minutes of diversion, if nothing else.

After all, Mom was gone. Mom was gone. Mom was gone. I cried as I reached for my pack of cigarettes and ran down the stairs to the parking lot and the 80-mile-per-hour drive to the hospital about 20 miles away.

But by the time I got to the hospital, the picture had improved slightly.

Mom was not gone. At least not yet.

Even though the preacher – "Padre" as I called him in those days when I wasn't really buying what he was selling – stood with my dad in the room; a private room, not the CCU. There was no breathing device jammed down her throat. No oxygen mask over her face. Just a deadly quiet.

There remained silent hope simply because Mom was twitching some.

The nurses finished putting in IVs. Not an easy task. Even unconscious, Mom grimaced slightly as the nurses forced needle into veins that had been collapsed by years of IVs, by years of fighting.

And Mom was breathing on her own...shallow, gasping, crackling breath filled with the textures of her disintegrating lungs.

I looked at my dad, my eyes asking if she was going to fool the black dog of death again.

He shrugged. The Padre was holding him up and praying.

Mom's eyelids began to fidget a bit.

I hugged my dad. I was preparing to say goodbye to my mother.

But what happened next made me smile in admiration at this woman who wasn't ready to go yet.

Her blue eyes slit slightly.

I sighed in relief. Mom had apparently fooled the docs that time, just as she had so many times before after being rushed to the hospital.

Eyes gradually opening fully, she focused in on me. Still too weak to talk, she smiled. Her eyes watered. Tears rolled down her cheeks.

"Not out of the woods, yet," the doctor cautioned.

But, you see, I knew better. I knew she'd bounce back. I knew my mom.

A day later she said, "I was dead. I saw the light. And then I was back. The first thing I saw was you standing by the bed."

I had to laugh. You take joy on its own terms.

Even when she said "I died and it wasn't so bad." I kept smiling because I knew she was going to go home.

She told me then she wasn't ready to die just yet. "I've still got to clean out that closet in the bedroom so your father won't have to do it.

"He's such a good man, putting up with all this nonsense."

Just then my wife, Suzanne, entered the room, our son, Joey — the second of two we've adopted from Romanian orphanages — in her arms.

Joey was quiet as he looked at his beloved "Nonny."

"Hello dears," Mom said, weakly.

"Nonny!" Joey almost screamed in joy. His mom rushed him out in the hallway, where the preacher waited.

"Sssshhh...we're in a hospital. You've got to be quiet," Suzanne told Joey, sternly, but warmly.

We all had to smile at Joey's reaction to seeing the woman the rest of the grandkids called "Nonna," but to him has been "Nonny" from the moment they met.

For some reason, he had taken to her just from the outset. Right off the plane from Romania he loved her.

Still does. Some time ago, he told me he wished I'd go ahead and die. It's not that he wanted me to suffer. "You can see Nonny. And you don't have to work so hard. I wish I could see Nonny."

I always tell him we'll see her soon enough. "Wouldn't

you miss me, Joey?"

"Yes. But you'd be with your mom like I'm with my mom."

He smiled at Suzanne. And I felt a little envy that his mom could smile back at him.

But to return to the time my mom saw the light and returned to clean out closets...

Almost a month after we all had rushed to the hospital to say goodbye, Mom was released from the hospital. Weaker, but in a way tougher, more determined not to die until she was ready.

At least not until the closets were cleaned out.

"I never thought it would come to this," Mom said, on a Sunday morning as I sat with her while my dad went to church.

"We worked so hard. We should be traveling, enjoying our money instead of spending it all on this." She shook her head in the direction of the small nightstand that had every drawer crammed with medicine and medical implements. Or the commode that was by the window. She confided the worst thing was not being able to get to the bathroom. "Damn, I'm going to get there, though..." She swore so seldom. Usually it was "gash" or some sort of derivative expletive. Maybe "crap" or "oh crap."

Only once in these long days did I hear her speak something stronger.

She wasn't feeling sorry for herself. She was just pissed off at the way she was, at the way the illness had gotten in the way of her dreams.

It wasn't too many respiratory therapy sessions before that the technicians had asked her to write down the things she missed most because of her illness. The first thing was

"Being able to play with my grandchildren…" Then she regretted not being able to go shopping for the holidays and birthdays she so relished celebrating.

Every child's birthday, every adult's birthday was an excuse for a family dinner and gathering for my mom. We called her "the birthday lady."

The final regret she wrote about was that she was trapped in her bed, unable to do things with Em (my dad), traveling, etc.

No wonder she hissed that expletive on that otherwise quiet Sunday.

That burst of proud, quiet anger was followed by the swallowing of more pills. I filled her nebulizer with the concoctions that were keeping her lungs working. And she leaned back in bed and sucked in the vaporized medicine, her pale, fearless blue eyes slitting to a near sleep.

The next day, Suzanne went to Mom's bedside to help her clean closets. Mostly Mom just talked, about her grandchildren and about her kids and about their wives…about places she had been and places she wished she could go with Dad, the "good man" she would be leaving sooner that she wished. The closets, by the way, remain filled.

CHAPTER THREE

Not even Sinatra helped this time

I thought of that time, just months earlier, often as I maintained my coffee-fueled stint at the hospital.

"She's not ready to die yet," I kept telling myself.

I had told her so many times during those long nights that I wasn't ready for her to go. I wasn't ready to grow up. I needed my momma. Still do.

A true Baby Boomer Baby...older than Elvis when he died; than John Lennon when he was gunned down by that little dweeb. And I'd outlived Jimi Hendrix, Janis Joplin, Jim Morrison and Jerry Garcia. But, baby, Frank Sinatra had kept on swinging well past 80 ...while Baby Boomer heroes had fallen.

Frank's long life provided me hope.

I found myself listening more to his songs...I'd always been a fan ever since hearing some of Dad's albums. I would use any sort of distraction to tell me I wasn't foolish for not being ready to say goodbye to my Mother.

Baby Boomers need to have parents...war brides and veterans of World War II, heroes, to baby them.

The kids of Frank's generation were tougher than those they spawned.

But then, as reality set in and I realized she was going to

die this time, that she'd outwitted her old nemesis and acquaintance devil death for her last time, I prepared to tell her the truth, to deliver the message I think she needed to hear.

I mean, I think a lot of the reason she kept fighting was because I told her she had to, that basically, the other option was unacceptable. To me. To her baby.

I knew that had changed. And someone needed to tell her.

I kind of sorted out my thoughts as I sat in the hospital parking lot and washed cigarette smoke down with thick coffee...

What would I say?

That I would miss her.

But she would always be with me.

My wife and kids loved her.

She could be with her own mom and dad; with her brother and sister, who had succumbed to the same disease so long ago.

She needed to be told it was okay now.

She was a religious person and believed in life after death.

She had convinced me that something had to be out there. Otherwise, what's the point?

Suzanne is deeply religious. And she felt my pain, my anguish as I thought through the message.

"I'm going to tell her now that it's okay," I told Suzanne the next afternoon, after I took a shower, hugged my kids and slipped into my Beatles T-shirt, cutoff blue jeans and dirty, white boat shoes to prepare for another night at the hospital with Dad.

And Mom.

I sent Dad off to get something to eat.

And I wandered down the hallway of the CCU, and into the palely lighted cubicle where Mom lay.

Quietly and alone, I stood in her room and told her it was okay now. I talked about heaven and the people she would see. In my mind, my Uncle Joe — her older brother who died more than 40 years earlier — was hugging her.

The little girl baby she had miscarried late in pregnancy — my little sister — was waiting for her, giggling.

Grandpa Champ was ready to embrace his baby daughter before thumbing the bowl of his clay pipe full of Prince Albert...from the can, of course.

Grandma Champ was slicing potatoes in the kitchen and getting ready to fry up a batch of perch from Walnut Lake.

Aunt Shirley was there, ready to pick on her baby sister.

Grandpa Ghianni, the tough and profane, old Italian immigrant would be there, maybe playing poker with Grandpa Champ. Taking a swig from his flask to wash down the raw eggs he so enjoyed rolled right out of the shell into his mouth, like oysters on the half shell.

Mom never really got along that well with Grandpa Ghianni. But then again, no one really did. We just loved him for who he was and what he had accomplished after crossing the Atlantic alone at age 12.

Mom would be glad to see Grandma Ghianni, whose sweet eyes would gleam at seeing her "Dotty" (pronounced with a heavy Italian accent, so it sounded almost like a song.)

Grandma Ghianni — who never shared with Mom the secret of her spaghetti sauce, saving that treat for "Emmy" (my dad) — finally would show her how to do it the Italian way.

Course, Mom had taught herself a recipe that Dad liked even better, but she wouldn't tell Grandma that. After all, there's probably room for a lot of spaghetti sauces in heaven. You might think angels preferred Alfredo sauce, but all they'd get from the Ghiannis would be Marinara.

These images raced through my sleep-deprived brain — about 8 hours in a week —as I leaned over the bed and ran my fingers through my mom's very thin, dry hair...

I kissed her forehead and rubbed her IV-scarred and fluid-swollen hand.

I knew what I had to say, and tears rolled.

"It's okay to stop fighting now, Mom...

"It's okay to die."

CHAPTER FOUR

'She's going now'

It was the next morning that my dad saw the light.

And about 20 hours after that, Dad came into the room I had hijacked at the end of the hospital corridor. For most of the nine nights she was in the hospital, I had slept there. Often I'd get up, tromp through the hospital; call Suzanne at home with a middle-of-the-night update. There always were tears in my wife's voice.

But she also gave me courage.

In my wanderings, I'd visit with the night nurses. I'd look in on my mom, with my dad sleeping at her bedside in a recliner. Sometimes I'd go downstairs for coffee. Maybe even step outside to indulge the habit I've now finally kicked...smoking. I'd listen to the sirens in the night; watch as the ambulances would unload traffic-accident carcasses at the ER. Sometimes I'd lean up against an ambulance and talk with the EMTs or deputies and share a smoke or two. I'd tell them why I was there, who was upstairs.

And these "hardened-by-seeing-too-much-death-and-sadness-after-midnight" fellows and young women would pat my shoulder. Everyone has a mom. Or had a mom.

No one ever wants to say goodbye to her.

No one's ever ready.

I'd snuff out my smokes and go back to "my room" and wait for the inevitable. Sometimes Dad would stop by and squeeze my toes or pat me in the middle of the night. It was quiet reassurance.

But this night, well, was different.

"Timmy," my dad said as he patted the left arm that was draped over my eyes. "Mother's having trouble."

Dad hadn't called me "Timmy" in probably 45 years.

Mom did sometimes. Most times it was Tim or Timothy (if I was in trouble). "Timothy Champ" if I truly had stunned her with my mischief. "Timothy Champ Ghianni," well, if I ever heard her say that, I knew there was some serious explaining to do.

After Dad called me "Timmy," I slipped from the bed and into my boat shoes. We walked down the hall, my arm over Dad's shoulders.

"Dad, you know her soul is already gone. She's in heaven," I muttered, trying to convince myself as much as him that this long battle actually was a victory...despite the fact that we knew she was dying, or at least the body was finally going to give up. And I wouldn't have a mom anymore.

We walked slowly back to Mom's bedside, where the CCU nurse was watching my mom's vital signs on the monitor, listening to her through a stethoscope and holding her wrist to check for any pulse.

"She's going now," said the nurse. "This is it. It may be seconds or it may be a half-hour."

Dad called his preacher – the Padre – and my brother as I clutched Mom's hand. I was frozen to her side. I couldn't leave as long as there was breath; as long as the machines beeped.

The monitors were slowed to almost nothing.

But there was still life.

"Her soul already has gone," I reminded myself and my dad when he came back into the room, clutching a Bible. "I know. It left when I saw the light," he said.

First he read her the 23rd Psalm.

Then he embraced her head. I leaned over and kissed her then him.

He held her head and said: "My Dotty, my beautiful Dotty. I'm going to miss you, Baby, Baby, Baby..."

Dad recited the Lord's Prayer. I caught up with him at the "hallowed be thy name" part.

At the end of the second time through the prayer, the nurse looked up at us.

"She's gone now."

Into the light.

"Oh, Baby, Baby, Baby, Baby...I'll always love you," Dad cried softly.

The Padre and my brother rushed into the room just as the nurse reached up and shut off the monitors, where no number showed, from which the beeping had stopped. She slipped from the room to give us a few moments of privacy, for goodbyes. Prayers.

And again, it was the 23rd Psalm. Then the Lord's Prayer. A few words from the preacher, I think about heaven and salvation.

After a few minutes, the nurse came back into the room and gently ushered us toward the door. "When you see her next, she'll look better."

She was talking about the magical powers of the mortician. But, of course, that wouldn't really be my mom. She'd been gone since Dad saw the light.

I preferred thinking about it that way. I knew that the next time I would see her again would be in heaven.

I looked back over my shoulder as they closed the blinds on the window and shut the door. They didn't want anyone looking in on the "death procedure" inside the CCU room.

I picked up the phone at the nurses' station to call Suzanne.

Then I went downstairs into cool, hazy predawn. Lighted a smoke. And cried.

I caught myself just as I was about to yell profanely into direction of the lightening horizon. Mom knew I cussed like a newspaperman. I remembered getting into trouble when I was 7 or so. There was an old cartoon show, "Huckleberry Hound" on at the time. In the theme song they played the name game, sort of, glorifying the hero by singing "Huckleberry, chuckleberry, duckleberry..." or something stupid like that, using different letters to make rhymes using the hound's name.

While singing along, I tried "F" at the beginning of the word.

Mom wasn't amused. She told me what I said was bad and not to do it again. Course, I didn't know back then that it was bad. But on this morning I knew what I was saying...

"Huckleberry," I said, or something like that. "My mom's dead."

CHAPTER FIVE

She wore her pink suit

The next few days were blurs of smiling faces and hugs; forced laughter and coffee choked down. There were funeral arrangements and flowers, trying to be strong for Dad as he picked out the most simple, yet elegant, coffin.

"Mom would like this," I told him.

There were poems, prayers and promises and many good-natured arguments with the Padre about why such a good woman would have suffered so long. Why would God permit this?

For years, I had spent my Sunday mornings at her house, sitting with Mom while Dad went to church. I had wavered from my strong religious upbringing. It just didn't make sense to me that she would be so sick. That she would suffer so. I told my mom that during those Sundays. She nodded, but added that someday I'd make sense of it.

"I hope you can," she added, always hesitant to agitate her smart-aleck son. "It would mean a lot to your dad if you'd have the children baptized. Me, too. I'll know."

"Shit, it means a lot to me, too," I'd tell her in my bravest, smark-alecky-ist manner. I knew cussing drew her ire. This time she laughed.

"Timothy Champ Ghianni, I don't know what I'm going

to do about you, my Sonny."

I related those comments to the Padre, who hugged me.

"At her side is where you needed to be, son. That was the right place," the preacher told me. Asked for an explanation as to why such a fine woman would die so miserably, he shrugged solemnly. "There are no answers. But you come to me and keep asking questions, any questions."

We buried her in the pink suit Dad bought her, but that she was never healthy enough to wear...tucked her in the pink shawl that was her favorite, something she'd gotten from her own mother. It was over her in the CCU room when she died. It was over her when she saw the light.

There was a picture of her cat Sophie in her hand.

My Aunt Rita — a devout Catholic — tucked a change purse "for the toll on the bridge" into the lining of the coffin. Or perhaps, knowing Rita, it may have been bingo money. I didn't know about a toll bridge to heaven, but Aunt Rita assured me there was. Guess I had better tell my kids about that someday, so they'll remember when it's time for me to pay the toll.

Aunt Rita also insisted Mom have good shoes on for all the walking she was going to do. That kind of made me smile. I didn't think they did a lot of walking in heaven. But, you know, if Mom was able to walk again without collapsing from lack of air, well that would be one of those heavenly gifts.

The funeral focused on Mom's passion for animals. "All Creatures Great and Small" was written on the program. Fittingly, a black bug crawled across the pulpit just as the pastor began his speechifying. "Normally, I'd have squashed it, killed that bug," he said, smiling. "Then I said 'What would Dot do?' The Padre lifted the bug from the pulpit and carried it to the side of the sanctuary, opening a door and setting it loose in the steamy September morning. "That is one of the lessons of the wonderful life of Dot Ghianni."

Her favorite hymns were sung: "How Great Thou Art" and "Amazing Grace." Both song titles are descriptive of the woman I called Mom.

My own wife held me tightly as we followed the casket from the sanctuary and helped Dad keep his balance.

Family, friends, in-laws, cousins, the Padre, others were at the grave as Mom's body was lowered. We left before the dirt was thrown atop her, because Dad didn't want to see that.

At his house afterward, some watched football. Others drank Chivas. Everyone ate the food that the church and funeral parlor and neighbors had sent over.

I mostly stood outside, drank coffee. Sometimes smoked. But mostly looked into the sun-punctuated sky.

Looking at Mom.

Looking for Mom.

Talking to Mom.

CHAPTER SIX

The shooting star and the bird

"I'll be okay now, Mom. Suzanne will take care of me. But I'm going to miss you."

Then I'd wink at heaven. And repeat the profanity. Over and over again.

I often puzzled during those talks to heaven about two incidents that happened in the hours and days after my mom had died. The first one came maybe 16 hours after her body gave out. I was outside with my dog, Buddy, and I was smoking a cigarette.

We live in the city, so sometimes you can't see the stars clearly. Seldom is it clear enough to see a "shooting star" through the urban haze of a hot summer night in Nashville. But there was one, tearing across the sky, as bright and clear as any I'd seen in my rambling days, back when I was camping in the Rockies while looking for America with an old pal of mine named "Wizard." The amazing clarity of meteors in the high country is never captured in the humid lowlands. Except that night when I was smoking with Buddy in the back yard. To be clear here: I was doing the smoking. Buddy was just there to offer emotional support.

When I told Suzanne about the shooting star, she said it was just Mom telling me she was okay, that everything was all right. Finally.

It was the next day, when Suzanne was filling the bird-feeders behind my mom's house — she loved all the creatures, remember — that a brightly feathered bird that none of us had ever seen before perched on the feeder. It stunned us. It made us smile.

The bird flew off over the tree line and toward heaven.

We never saw it, or any bird resembling it, again.

CHAPTER SEVEN

She finally saw the light

A few days after the funeral, I drove my dad to the doctor, the same doctor who had struggled for years to keep my mom alive.

Dad's blood pressure was out-of-whack. He was dizzy and, of course, depressed.

Dad grabbed my knee as we drove down Interstate 65 to the Franklin, Tennessee, exit that leads to the doctor's office, just behind the hospital where Mom died.

He was silent. Then the rising sun shone on his face as Dad looked over at me.

"There was another prayer Mom always used to say, something about going to sleep and the soul. I can't remember it. Do you?"

I smiled even as tears began to stream down my face.

It was the prayer that Mom taught us as she tucked my brother, Eric, and me in each night, a prayer I'm sure taught by millions of moms.

"Now I lay me down to sleep, I pray the Lord my soul to keep. If I should die before I wake I pray the Lord my soul to take."

Dad sobbed. "That's it. Tim, could you write that down for me sometime?"

Consider it done, Dad.

After my dad's checkup, I took him home. And I decided to drop by the cemetery before going downtown to the newspaper office.

Mom had been a newspaperwoman, by the way. So had Suzanne. Both gave up those jobs for the harder and more-fulfilling — at least so they both have told me — jobs of raising children, running a house, caring for a husband.

I'm sure it's a harder job. I'm not sure about the fulfilling part. I'd hate to be raising me. Hate to be married to me, too. Both tasks have proven difficult.

On this very steamy September day, I pulled the little Toyota Tercel — with its long-dead air-conditioner — to the curb along the cemetery's main drive. I rolled up the windows, climbed out and slowly shuffled up the hilltop under the tree that shaded Mom's fresh grave. The graveside was still covered with the wilting floral arrangements from the funeral.

"Hi Mom, it's Tim," I said, focusing on the ground, then realizing that I really needed to be looking up and at the billowing clouds.

Lawnmowers roared someplace across the green expanse of the cemetery. There was a police siren in the distance.

I kneeled down to pick up a stone, a white pebble, and rolled it over my fingers. I dropped it onto the red soil and instead grabbed a wilted flower, a lily of some sort, from one of the arrangements. Mom liked lilies and daffodils.

I slowly stood upright.

Standing in the shade cast by the tree onto that patch of barren ground, six feet above the casket and heaven's distance from her departed soul, I decided it was time to write this story of the woman who had disappeared from the Earth, the woman who lived with amazing grace and dignity.

The woman who finally saw the light.

It was the same tale I had told her the night before my dad saw the light.

What follows is the story I told her, a story burned in my mind by trauma of having first told my mom it was okay to leave me.

It was okay to die.

CHAPTER EIGHT

Love just came spilling out

"Hi Mom, it's Tim."

"You're looking better tonight," I said beside her hospital bed. "Your vital signs all look improved." I lied as I looked from the blinking machines in the Critical Care Unit.

She squinted slight recognition.

I'd been in here many times in the days before, talking to her when she could recognize me, making her promise to me that she would get out of the hospital. "I still need my mom," I'd tell her.

"I'm not ready to say goodbye."

"I'm going home," she whispered one night. "But I'm going to need a lot of help, Tim. A lot of help. Your father can't do it all."

She looked around the dimly lighted CCU room, where just a day or so before they had pulled the ventilator out of her lungs, allowing her to breathe on her own; to fight on her own.

And, although we didn't accept it yet, removing the ventilator allowed her to die on her own. There was no machine doing the breathing for her. And she simply could no longer do the breathing for herself. She was on the pathway to death, but under her own power and at her own will. She just needed to know it was okay.

Anyway, we were still talking about life, about the future, about the kids on this night. Or I was talking. She was listening.

Then she asked me to go wake my father, who was grabbing a couple of hours in the bed I'd confiscated down the hall in the hospital.

"Dad, Mom needs you," I said softly shaking his shoulder.

He bolted upright, fear in his eyes.

"No, she's okay right now," I assured him. "She just needs to see you."

His unstated question answered, he wandered through the corridors to the room where his life's mate waited.

"I'm scared, Em," she said.

"I'm not ready and I'm scared."

He hugged her.

I left them, arm-in-arm, as much passion in their eyes as they ever felt, I'm sure.

As the hours passed, others came to visit. Their intentions were good. I let them take my spot by her right side. Mom didn't have time to waste. Nor did she figure she needed to sugar-coat anything. She waved them off, wiggled her finger to me to come back to her side.

I stroked her hand as she closed her eyes, occasionally whispering loud enough to be heard over the beeping machine.

But as her fight wore on and her battling body wore down, I knew it was time to talk to her. I'd already told her it was okay if she wanted to die. But now I just wanted to tell her, one last time on Earth, what she meant to me, to us all ...while she could still hear me.

So, I took a deep breath, thought about what I would say, or at least how I would start. And this monologue of memories and love just came spilling out...

CHAPTER NINE

'Remember me when you get to the Pacific Ocean'

It's just like that old Jimmy Stewart movie, Mom... "It's a Wonderful Life."

Only this time, you're George Bailey.

You've touched us all in so many ways, touched so many people.

If it wasn't for you, Emily and Joe would have never gotten out of the orphanages in Romania.

Just think of the Ghianni kids they may bring into the world.

Or perhaps, because of the simple lessons of kindness I got from you, they'll go back sometime and help some of the children in Romania in some way.

But I'm getting ahead of myself here...really not prepared to deliver a speech. No notes here. Just wanted to remind you of a good life, well lived. "And in the end, the love you take is equal to the love you make." An old Beatles line, from when they said goodbye. You always made fun of my love of The Beatles.

I had other heroes.

Remember Davy Crockett's cabin?

That's one of my first memories of all the trips you and

Dad took us on as we were growing up.

I don't remember too much about it except that Eric dropped the wooden bar on the inside of the door and locked me and him in the cabin and the park ranger had to crawl in the window to get us out. I also remember thinking it pretty cool that here we were at the home of the guy who was every little boy's TV hero back then. King of the Wild Frontier.

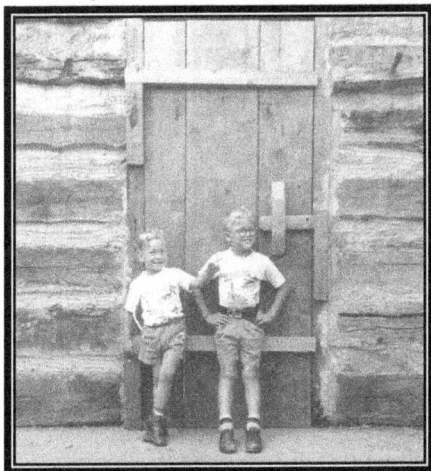

My coonskin cap was on the shelf by the back window of the car.

Killed him a B'ar when he was only 3.

You wouldn't have liked that, would you? As much as you love animals. Whatever did that old B'ar do to Davy?

My memories of that trip are slight. I guess I was only 3, myself. No B'ar killing. Heck, I may have been 4.

I do remember some things about that journey that took us from our house at 1812 Beverly Road in Sylvan Lake, Michigan, to Washington, D.C., and then into the South; weird things, or odd things, anyway.

Like the fact that you kept plastic cups in the back seat so Eric and I could pee and we wouldn't have to stop. We'd just throw it out the window.

Of course, that was long before the days of the interstates, so you never knew where the next stop was going to be.

We wound through what are now called "blue highways,"

in reference to the fact they now are just represented on road maps by thin, blue lines among the thick yellow and red of the major interstates and freeways of today. But back then, these were the major thoroughfares of our country.

Highway 41. Down on Highway 61, Highway 70, Route 66. Well, I guess we didn't hit that last one on this trip. I did that later in life when I traveled with my friend Wizard after college graduation.

You took curious joy out of the fact I went on the quest for America. I wonder whatever happened to Old Wizard, anyway?

I've a curious habit of closing doors behind me as I pass through life. Sometimes it's good as I leave baggage behind. Other times, well, there are friends like Wizard who somehow just vanish.

Remember Wiz and I started on the day after we went to see Elvis down at Municipal Auditorium in Nashville? You bought the tickets for me during the spring before I graduated, to make sure I'd get to see him.

Anyway, I have plenty of time to relive that trip in search of America, a quest in a 1965 Falcon for the kindness and respect that surely were a part of what made this country great in the first place; the compassion that brought the immigrants.

That 1973 trip, if it did anything, assured me that the real heart and soul of America is in the diners and the taco stands, the all-night casinos and truck stops, the 30-cents-per-gallon gas jockeys who cleaned the windshield and checked the oil for free, as part of the job.

It was the kindly doctor, Dr. Gutierrez, who cleaned and stitched up a deep wound in my calf muscle, the result of a minor accident. He charged me nothing. His office was someplace between nowhere and Carlsbad. The waiting room was filled with faces of brown and reddish hues. And this weary white boy with the throbbing leg.

"You get back on the highway and find America," he told me, shaking off offers of money. "Remember me when you get to the Pacific Ocean."

I passed by crying Indian babies in the waiting room as I headed back to the highway. Doctor's orders: Go find America. I wish I remembered his first name.

That's a different story. But really they are all interwoven. You taught me to seek out the best in people, because they are worth it.

My love of the road is deep and liberating. I still like driving, even though Suzanne thinks I'm the world's worst driver. You're gonna have to talk to her about that, since you taught me how to drive. That love of negotiating the two-lane blacktops was born on our family vacations.

Course, I don't make my kids pee in cups. There's always a McDonald's or a rest stop coming up around the next bend nowadays.

CHAPTER TEN

We had our heads shaved

During our family's summer journey to the South in the mid-1950s, I have vague memories of seeing Robert E. Lee's dead horse or something like that. It was at a college somewhere. Behind bars. I'm sure it's there. Really. At least it's trapped in my mind. An odd thing to remember.

In Lexington, Kentucky, we saw the horse-breeding stables where champions are reared. I remember being impressed that they slept standing up.

But this trip — that included seeing the Lincoln Memorial and Washington Monument, Davy Crockett's cabin and a Confederate hero's dead horse — is best remembered because of ringworm.

Remember we stopped at a roadside motel. Again, 45 years ago, there weren't too many Holiday Inns. The motels all had little cabins or rooms where you could back the trunk right up to the front door. This one was kind of like The Bates Motel that Anthony Perkins ran in "Psycho."

But, of course, we weren't scared. It was fun. All motels were like that back then. This one was just a little more rural.

I remember the old, black steam locomotive that billowed thick smoke as it rolled right behind the motor hotel, wrapping itself around the mountain as it ascended into the misty heights of the Smokies. I was so impressed by the "Whoo-Whoo" of the steam horn and the rolling clouds of black smoke filling the sky.

Back to the ringworm.

You always thought Eric and I got ringworm at that motel.

I remember when we got home, we had to have our heads shaved for the ringworm treatment. And Eric had to wear a nylon stocking on his head when he went to school. I wasn't school-age yet, so I saved you that embarrassment.

Of course, ringworm wasn't uncommon back in those days. But it was — still is, I guess — something that is blamed on filth, on unsanitary conditions.

You always kept the house immaculate.

And your children were always scrubbed fresh and dressed well, when we were struggling on Dad's $3,000 teacher and coach's salary, that he supplemented by delivering beer kegs in the summer.

I bet you were mortified to send Eric to school in that stocking.

And glad you could keep me and my shaved, nylon-covered head in the house on Beverly Road.

CHAPTER ELEVEN

Chickens with their heads cut off

Remember when Rusty Parry and I ate the tulips by the house in Sylvan Lake? You always laughed at me for doing that. Truth is, they tasted good. I haven't eaten a tulip since, but those were the best darned tulips ever. Ruined your garden that year, but at least we didn't die.

Or the time that Rusty and I went to the big drainage ditch or canal that led to the lake? It was straight-down and deep. But we didn't know that. All we knew was it was cool to park our tricycles by the side of the ditch and roll downhill on our sides, getting as close to the water as we could. You caught us doing that. Good thing, too. I never told you, but our eventual plan was to ride the tricycles down the hill. Truly cool.

I know you taught me to swim early.

I can't remember if Rusty knew how to swim yet.

But chances are neither one of us were prepared for the Evel Knievel Ride, full speed downhill and into the dark water.

You probably saved our lives when you caught us. But you didn't save our butts. Well, in my case, it was my finger you hit with the switch as you chased us back to the house. I had my hand over my rear end as we ran through the yard of the guy who used to let us watch the chickens dance after he cut off their heads.

Strange I'd remember that now. Again, something you didn't approve of. But those chickens sure danced around. Like chickens with their heads cut off.

Anyway on our flight from the drainage ditch you ran full speed. It's amazing to see you now and then remember how you could run, especially when I was in trouble. You caught Rusty just as he was screaming "You can't spank me. You're not my mommy."

He was proven wrong about the first part of his argument when the switch tagged his bottom.

Remember, I had my hand in the way, so it was there that you caught me with the switch. And you had to take me to the doctor to check out my swollen finger. You figured you'd be accused of child abuse.

I can't remember how the tricycles got home. Maybe the guy who cut the heads off the chickens brought them.

CHAPTER TWELVE

'I bit him back'

Yes, Mom, you were strict. And you raised us so well. And you touched so many lives.

But you also were always quick with phrases, some of them inherited from your Pop. Like if a mosquito bit me, you'd tell me, "Well, just bite him back."

Remember when I was in first grade and you and I were walking down Madison Street in Grand Rapids, near where my teacher, Mrs. Spoor lived. I'll never forget her. I guess you never forget your first-grade teacher.

I imagine she's long gone now. Of course, she seemed so much older then, back when I was 5 or 6.

I remember it was kind of a cloudy summer day and Mrs. Spoor was working in her front yard and she came over to the sidewalk to visit as we stopped. You both were surprised to see me suddenly pulling my left forearm to my mouth, chomping down and spitting something on the sidewalk.

"What was that?" you asked.

"A mosquito," I said. "I bit him back."

You had to explain to Mrs. Spoor that I was simply following my mother's directions.

CHAPTER THIRTEEN

'Just good old Americans'

I'll always remember the day you came looking for me and Jimmy Haan. We were in Garfield Park. This was long before the days when people stopped letting their kids wander the city streets because of the beasts in human form out there. But it was a summer evening. And Jimmy and I told you we were going down to the Malt Shop on Burton Street. There we spent many pleasant hours, ordering malts and playing the jukebox.

Elvis and the Everly Brothers were my favorites in the three-plays-for-a-quarter jukebox.

I remember playing a syrupy Everly tune called "That's Old-Fashioned" for my 9-year-old girlfriends.

I always liked the girls.

If we ran out of money for malts, because of our generosity with the jukebox, Jimmy and I would resort to a trick we saw in the television commercials for the old product called "Fizzies." They were these little, fizzy, fruit-flavored tablets that you drop in a glass of water and soon the water tasted putridly sweet. We liked the purple best. I suppose it was grape or something vaguely like grape. Lots of times we had to substitute Fizzies for our preferred 25-cent chocolate malted if we were trying to dazzle our girls with our jukebox heroes.

"Could I have a glass of water, please?" we'd ask the guy behind the counter in the white T-shirt, apron and paper hat. We were repeating the line from the old TV commercial for Fizzies. He'd give us the water and we'd have our drinks. I don't suppose he'd put up with it except for the fact that we were "regulars." If we had money to spare, we'd blow it on jukebox songs, malteds and lime phosphates.

I remember taking Jimmy Haan there to the Malt Shop after I lost by two votes in my attempt to be elected captain of the Dickinson Elementary School safety patrol. Jimmy'd been my campaign manager. The consolation was that I became lieutenant.

You gave my campaign manager and me a dollar and told us to go get ourselves chocolate malteds. Nobody sells malteds anymore, do they? It's just milkshakes as the Golden Arches have taken over America.

Anyway, back to Garfield Park. That one day, Jimmy and I went down to the Malt Shop on our Schwinn bikes. And on the way, we began stopping at Coke machines. There were many more of them around back then, dispensing those old 7-ounce bottles for a dime. We'd check the bottle-cap compartment, the little container beneath the bottle opener, for the discards. These were like coins to us. So we started on an urban adventure, roaming from corner to corner, grocery to gas station, putting the bottle caps in little sacks.

The big, bald guy at the Sinclair station laughed at us as he looked up from the grease rack.

"Help yourself, Timmy," he hollered. Seemed like we knew everybody. I imagine you and Dad did business there.

Our bottle caps collected, Jimmy and I went to our favorite hiding place, deep in the bushes at Garfield Park, to divide up the "loot." The sun was going down. It was midsummer, so it was likely after 8. We'd lost track of time.

You didn't. As usual, you were home, alone, with Dad out on the road selling water heaters during the week. Your responsibility was your kids and the house.

We didn't really think we were doing anything remotely punishable until you burst into our hiding place in the bushes with a switch in your hand. We also didn't know you knew our hiding place.

You chased us home, never once raising the switch. I wonder, with all this talk of switches, if people even know what they are any more, these thin, green branches plucked fresh off a tree; plenty of spring in them for stinging the bottom of a wayward child.

But that evening, I remember you laughing at us as we ran away from you and that switch...directly into the unlocked front door at 507 Elliott Street.

And Jimmy Haan spent the night at our house.

You let us climb out from your bedroom window and onto the roof over the TV room and look at the stars. "Look for the Big Dipper, boys," you said.

I also remember you helping us gather bottle caps when we would ride with you to the grocery.

Remember when we'd surprise you by climbing in your trunk on grocery day?

Back then, there was a little latch inside every trunk that you could use to open it from the inside. I have no idea if there is such an "escape latch" anymore, because I no longer ride in trunks. Besides that, someplace between those trunk-riding days and now, I developed severe claustrophobia.

My kids better not take trunk-riding up, either.

We got quite a big laugh the first time or two we huddled in the trunk waiting for you to open it to load up your groceries...only to find a couple of stinky little boys.

I think the last time we did that, you told us to walk home from the A&P. Obviously you were scared we'd suffocate in the summer-heated trunk of the Chevy.

I shouldn't be talking about this.

Wouldn't want word to get back to Emily and Joey. Nor would I want them climbing around on my cars like you let us climb on the roof, the hood, wherever, on the old '51 brown-on-brown sedan.

We'd play Army on it while it was parked in the driveway. Your only rule was that we take our shoes off, so we didn't scratch it. That metal was hot on bare feet in the summer, but the imaginary adventures were worth it.

Anyway, back to the last time you caught us in the trunk. When you dispatched Jimmy and me away from the grocery store parking lot for the seven or eight-block walk home, you didn't know that the path of shamed trunk refugees took us through our favorite vacant lot, just behind a body shop. There was a steep hill there. During the winter it was our sledding hill. All the kids would pack it down and throw buckets of water on it to ice it to dangerously slick proportions.

But this was summer. And often we'd find skeletons of cars in various stages of disrepair and disassembly behind the shop.

It didn't take us long to figure out that it was great fun to jam the gearshifts to neutral and push these engine-less monsters to the edge of the hill, climb in and ride down the hill, laughing.

Usually, we could get other kids to help us push it back uphill if we'd promise to let them ride along.

I think this is probably the first time I've told you that.

But you know, I've always told you a lot about myself. If anyone was non-judgmental about the way I have lived my life it was you, Mom.

It's like when I told my friends that you'd asked me if I had ever indulged in the substances all Baby Boomers seemed to try, at least if they were in school during The Beatles, Summer of Love, Days of Rage times. My times.

And I answered "yes."

You told me it wasn't a good thing to do and warned me against drugs. Still you never condemned me. You would prefer that I talk to you rather than hide.

And when I did falter — you understood. You talked to me. And I told you about how it feels to be so all alone, a complete unknown; that you feel like you must get stoned.

You also were so pleased when I married Suzanne. In so many ways she reminds me of you. She has dreams and goals. She's a newspaperwoman. She loves people and animals. She loves kids.

Alcohol really has no part in our lives, except for the occasional glass of red wine at Thanksgiving. She can't drink because of blood pressure. I don't drink because I found out how important it is to feel your own pain and deal with it soberly. I'm probably in a lot of ways afraid to drink, too.

I mean, it was fun at times. Too much fun. I still relish the feel of alcohol rolling down my throat, that glorious burn. But mostly I relish it in my memories and have a Diet Coke instead.

Of course, I was a full-grown man when we talked about those things...past the switching ages and stages.

If I'd been smoking pot back in the '50s, where this story begins, I probably would have been taken to the doctor by a mom who was afraid of being labeled a child-abuser. An angry and loving woman who totes a switch.

It didn't strike me until later that as a young woman — a collegian in the early 1940s, who'd married a war-bound GI and then went on to become a cop reporter in Chicago during the war years — that you'd probably been exposed to a lot of things that were truly awful. So any of my admissions didn't startle you.

I do remember that you told me "Scumbag" by John Lennon and Frank Zappa was a bit offensive. But even my general taste in music was encouraged.

You liked it that I spent my allowance — money earned by cutting the lawn, shoveling the snow or taking out the trash — on 45s. Usually I could get them for a nickel apiece from Tommy LaGordo, whose dad owned that beer joint up near Madison Heights, just at the edge of what was then called "the colored neighborhood." Not by you, mind you. You'd have tongue-lashed anybody who used that term.

You always used the term "Negro." It was the accepted term when you were raising kids.

I know it's been tough for you to change your vocabulary and call then "black." That was as derogatory as "colored" back then. And you refuse to call anyone "African-American." "They are as American as anyone else," you explained. "Just good old Americans."

Anyway, Tommy LaGordo would take the jukebox discards and sell them to me. I've still got them. Yes Mom, I'm a pack rat.

Just ask Suzanne about that.

CHAPTER FOURTEEN

Let the music play

You and Dad would sneak dollars into my wallet so I could buy music.

When you turned 40, you and Dad had a big party in the living room of the house in Grand Rapids.

Eric and I stood at the railing and watched as you and Dad played my 45s — Elvis, Chubby Checker, Fats Domino, Duane Eddy, Bobby Darin and Chuck Berry — while dancing with your friends. I remember you all doing the limbo under a broomstick as you played Chubby's "Limbo Rock."

You also took me to the store when I bought my first LP — Elvis' "Blue Hawaii." I think the store was called Arland's or something like that. It cost $2 to buy that album. Rock A Hula Baby. I've still got that, too.

The cover, with Elvis in a Hawaiian shirt, helped inspire me to wear similar bright shirts throughout my adult life.

You helped me when I decided that in fourth grade I wanted to be Elvis for Halloween. We rinsed my hair jet black. Got a pair of Dad's WWII infantry combat boots and polished them deep, shiny black. Filled the toes up with newspapers to keep my feet from coming out. You reversed the lining on a sport coat bought at a thrift store so the satin sheen was on the outside. You spray-painted a toy guitar with gold-flake paint.

And now, Mom, as I look at you, I want to sing you "Love Me Tender." But of course, I can't sing. And I know I'll have to let you go.

If I have one interest in life other than my family and writing, it is in music. Thank you, Mom.

Of course, I talked earlier a little about how you always have kidded me about how The Beatles influenced me, how I grew my hair long when The Beatles played Ed Sullivan and how I've seldom had it short since.

Well, I did get it cut for football when I was in high school, but that's another story. And I did get it cut to "respectable" length when I graduated from Iowa State. Two years growth fell on the floor of the barber shop down by the old campus cigar store and just a few doors downhill from where I hung out with Black Panthers and Black Muslims in an attempt to learn. On the way downstairs from that first meeting with the Muslims, I walked in front of the record shop. The Rolling Stones "Let It Bleed" album was too good to pass up on the day.

CHAPTER FIFTEEN

Birmingham and The Stones

Back to the hair and what you would say to me…

"You're stuck in the '60s," you'd tell me. But you'd laugh. When you were stronger, you were the only one I'd let cut my hair. You remember back when Eric and I were kids in Sylvan Lake and Dad would give us buzz cuts? My hair will be that short again, I suppose…when I get older, losing my hair, many years from now.

Suzanne cuts my hair now. I promise Mom, that I'll be getting it cut real soon. You've heard that before haven't you?

Remember it was just a couple of years ago that you encouraged me to ride with a buddy, Jay Orr, a music writer from the old Nashville Banner, down to Birmingham, Alabama, to see The Rolling Stones.

"They may never play here again. To you, they are like old friends. You need to go," you said. "They are pretty old. Course you are, too. I saw Mick, and what's that other boy's name? Keith. They were on the Today Show the other morning. They looked all grown up. Show business sure takes a toll on people, doesn't it?

"Journalism, too, I guess." You joked me whenever you could about all the deep lines in my face, the dark eye circles and my flowing, white hair. Emily tells me I look like George

Washington, Mom.

Anyway, you told me I needed to go see The Stones. "They'd be like old friends of yours. The Rolling Stones, The Beatles, even Bob Dylan all grew up with you. Good or bad."

You of course were trying to goad me into saying something that we could "discuss" about The Beatles and The Stones. You always liked those conversations. "How did they help you and your friends stop the war in Vietnam and what good came of it?" That sort of thing. Mom and son discussions blowin' in the wind.

But you also were glad that I went to Birmingham that night to see The Stones. I stood on a hill in the black section of Birmingham and paid a guy $5 to watch Jay's old Toyota. It was sort of like a protection racket, I suppose. Another $2 bought me a beer and the right to use his outside restroom.

You laughed when I told you this.

But you thought it was particularly special that when Jay rounded a curve in the road, only to see a red fox, he nearly wrecked his old Toyota.

At 4 a.m., country roads belong to foxes, not 45-year-old retired hippies who still can't get no satisfaction.

I see you smile now, Mom. You like it when I make fun of myself. Or maybe you are smiling because I'm talking about saving the life of a little fox. Or perhaps the fact that I choose friends who also care about foxes.

The fox is important in what I'm telling you tonight, because you taught me compassion. For all creatures great and small, you used to say.

If you ever have to have a grave marker, that should be on it. "All creatures great and small..." Me? I'll use that old Dylan lyric: "There must be some kinda way outta here."

Your closed eyes are smiling now, Mom.

CHAPTER SIXTEEN

Easing the pain in our hearts

I guess the fox story now takes me to your pets; our pets. We always had cats at the house.

You've told me that you started your animal collecting when you left Fort Ord, Dad's final stop before he shipped out to the Philippines in 1945. Anyway, you had gotten married in Texas. Tyler, Texas, I think. I can't remember what fort or camp. You'd set up housekeeping there and in a couple more places...Riverside, California, near Pasadena, and then up at Fort Ord.

While you were in California, you adopted that little kitten, Blossom, a red cat.

You know I have a red cat, too. Pal is his name. He's really pink, not red.

Anyway, when your second lieutenant husband climbed aboard a ship bound for Manila or wherever, it was time for you to move back to the Midwest. Your destination was Chicago, where you went to work for the newspaper. Accompanying you on that trip was Blossom. I think you said she was in a box in the baggage car.

You said the worst thing about that trip was that you had to get off the train in St Louis for a day or two to make way for troops and troop trains. "Gash. No place hotter that St.

Louis in the summer," I recall you saying.

Anyway, Blossom had Junior. Then Blossom died of rat poisoning in Sylvan Lake, maybe from the barn where that guy liked to make dead, headless chickens dance.

I remember Junior. There are pictures of me with him someplace in your house. I don't remember how he died. I think he just disappeared... probably poisoned, too.

Then there was Goldie, another red kitten, who disappeared.

But mostly, of all your red cats, I remember Ginger. He was in your house almost as long as I was. Ginger lived for 17 years, plus.

I remember you scolding Ginger when he'd get up in the elm trees in Grand Rapids and go after the birds. I also remember you trying to help him escape when the blue jays turned the tables on him, beginning their own attack, Ginger howling.

I guess it wasn't long after Ginger brought home his last dead bird that you decided cats belonged in the house. You hated to see dead things.

And here I am talking to my mom, a most precious person who helped shape me. And I don't know how long I'm going to have you to talk to.

You always said that's what animals taught us. They died, helping to ease the pain in our hearts when people died.

The compassion you taught me carried me through my life so far.

Remember when I used to go to the dog shelter after school?

It was a few blocks from Dickinson Elementary, in Grand Rapids, where we moved after Dad left teaching to go into the water heater business. The dog shelter also was very near that hill where Jimmy and I would ride the junk cars downhill in the summer and speed down, out of control, on the icy slopes in winter.

Anyway, after school, Jimmy and I would stare in the windows or go inside the dog shelter and just look at the puppies. We wouldn't ignore the discarded older dogs, either.

You said you didn't want a dog, because they'd be too much work and that you'd end up having to care for the dog even if I promised I would.

"Mom, what would happen if a dog followed me home one day?" I often asked. And you know, I often tried to coax a stray to follow me. Even tried to get that black, fuzzy dog from up Elliott Street to move home with me once. I can't remember the people's names. I just remember the sidewalk in front of their house encircled a massive elm tree. Must have been poured back in the days when cities went out of their ways to save trees instead of chop them down. Back to the black, shaggy dog. Those neighbors wouldn't have appreciated their dog being taken, I suppose. Nice dog, though.

Anyway, you finally gave in. On my 10th birthday you gave me Lassie, a Shetland Sheepdog (miniature collie). She was beautiful and sweet. Her papers gave her the name "Timmy O'Lassie." Lassie caught distemper when she went to the vet to be spayed. It almost killed her as a pup. It ended up as a long death sentence. Put her to sleep, the vet recommended at the time.

We took her home.

And beautiful Lassie fought hard, just like you have all these years.

The main remnant of her disease was that she became an epileptic. Seizures would strike any time. Of course, we would medicate her when she was done with her "fits." But when she was in the throes of grand mal seizure we'd just have to pet her, console her; a pencil in her mouth, above her tongue, to keep her from biting it off or swallowing it down. When she'd come to her senses, we'd tell her it was okay. She was obviously upset because during the fits, this well-behaved dog always urinated all over the place. She was afraid she'd be in trouble.

All she got was love.

Holding her after her fits, helping with her medication taught me a lot about illness...about degenerating, debilitating illness. But Lassie taught me about the trauma of seeing something or someone you love in misery. I had always wanted a dog. And here is this precious baby who wanted to live, but needed help, needed encouragement.

Love. Faith. Hope. Death.

It was a lesson I've leaned on in recent years, particularly just the other day when I watched the doctors work to bring you back to life on the table in the Emergency Room downstairs.

Because Lassie was so ill, we took her everywhere we went. She was a well-traveled dog. She went to Niagara Falls more than once. She even traveled with us on our two-week journey out to the Black Hills of South Dakota, where she saw buffalo, wild burros and Indians on those poverty-stricken reservations.

She visited Deadwood, where Wild Bill Hickok was shot in the back and she also went to Mount Rushmore.

I'm guessing that not too many Midwestern house dogs saw the sights of the Wild, Wild West.

I remember you would take our baby shirts and put them on her in the winter time, so she wouldn't get cold — she was a weak animal. But well dressed.

When I was a senior in high school, we took her with us when we went to visit the University of Michigan, where I was thinking of going to school, where I already had been accepted.

After all, that was where you and Dad met; where you returned after the war when Dad was working on his master's.

But on that day, Lassie was so sick we couldn't stay long at the school.

We got back in the car and began the drive back to the Chicago suburbs, where we lived then.

Somewhere around Benton Harbor, Michigan, I was sleeping in the back of the car, with Lassie sleeping with her head on my sleeve. "Timmy, your dog is dying," you said, shaking me. You reached back and stroked her. I stroked her, too.

"It's okay Lassie. It's okay. I'll always love you."

I was wearing my high school letter jacket. In her dying gasp, a dribble of blood came from Lassie's mouth. I never cleaned that jacket. The blood stain remains on the leather sleeve 30-some years later. I couldn't and wouldn't clean it.

We cried all the way home. It was the most somber journey of my life.

At least up until the journey that I think is going to come up sometime soon. Or the journey that I am sharing with you already.

It wasn't two weeks after Lassie died that I came in the house after running to the local discount house to buy The Beatles so-called "White Album" and The Rolling Stones "Beggars Banquet." I always liked to buy Beatles or Stones records on the day they came out, if possible.

Remember, it was you and Dad who bought me the 45 RPM recording of "I Wanna Hold Your Hand" the day after the Fabs were on Ed Sullivan?

Anyway, when I carried the two albums into the family room of our house, you were there. Dad was there. And so was this little black and white Shetland Sheepdog we named Misty or really Maid Melissa of the Highlands. Smartest dog I ever knew. Just as Lassie was my 10th birthday present, Misty was my 17th.

I got to know her as The Beatles sang about "Rocky Raccoon" and "Bungalow Bill" and The Stones preached about "Sympathy for the Devil."

After we got Misty a new tradition was begun.

When I would get off the school bus at the end of the day, you'd be sitting beneath the big ash tree in front of our house at 61 Ellendale in Deerfield, Illinois, just outside Chicago. And you'd let Misty loose just as I was approaching the corner, so she would jump up and greet me.

So, up until now in this adventure, we'd just had one dog at a time in the house.

That would change.

The first step in the growth of what eventually became your beloved pack of dogs came when Eric graduated from college a couple of years later...1971.

I went to the animal shelter to buy him a puppy. Instead I saw this sweet, older dog in a pen of puppies. It was a fluffy dog, kind of like the one I tried to coax away from the neighbors' house in Grand Rapids, the house with the elm in the middle of the sidewalk.

"She's too sweet to be around the bigger dogs," the folks at the Orphans of the Storm dog rescue agency told me. "The other dogs pick on her, so we had to put her in with the puppies. A family took her home the other day, but brought her back because they wanted a watch dog. She's not that. She's just a love dog."

Well, all you need is love, as some of my old friends used to sing.

Soon, the dog that was to be named Izzy was in the back seat of the '65 Falcon Futura and en route to your house.

It was Eric's dog. But he never really took her from your house.

What a beautiful dog. Eric said her name "Izzy" was short for "Insipid." You said it was short for "Isobel." You won out. You called her Isobel until her dying day, a day I had to be there for when she was given the final injection after a fight with cancer some 15 or so years later.

Izzy outlived Misty, but not by much. I had held Misty when she died a year or so before.

But those were just two of your dogs.

Remember when you had five dogs living in the house here in Nashville?

Of course, there were Misty and Izzy.

Then after Grandma Champ died and Grandpa moved in with you and Dad, he brought his dog, Spuddy, the beagle mix that was shaped like a nice baked potato.

But even before that you'd found that big golden retriever eating trash by the side of the interstate during a fierce thunderstorm.

You and Dad got him in the car and took him home.

You kept him in the garage at first. But I told you then that you had another dog.

You didn't say anything.

You had an ad in the paper under the "found dog" heading. But I think you were glad when no one called to claim the dog you later named Stormy.

It was Dad's favorite dog ever, I think.

Of course, you weren't done. One day, the neighbor dogs — who were allowed to roam freely — chased a black-and-white beagle/hound mix to your doorstep and then stood at the foot of the brick stairs, barking and growling while the little fella cowered and scratched at the door.

You let him in the house.

Bongo never left. I have a suspicion he became your favorite.

In any case, that upped the dog population to five.

And then there were the cats.

After you moved to Nashville from Chicago, Ginger died. He's buried in a tool box in the woods up behind your house.

A friend gave you a kitten that you named Topsy after one of your mom's dogs, who was named after the character that "just grew" in "Uncle Tom's Cabin."

But there was that other cat whose yellow eyes caught the light from your family room every night.

He'd stare in. You didn't want another animal at the time. After all, you had a pretty good four-legged population in the house already.

But you put food out for the old stray.

"Those are the eyes of Satan," you'd joke when the yellow eyes shined in from the pitch-black of your wooded back yard.

At night, we'd hear the tomcat fights in the woods behind the house.

You'd get me up and we'd go look for your "stray." Usually he was fine. One time he had a gash on his neck, you took him to the vet and had him stitched up, before letting him continue his roustabout ways.

The time he came to the back door with only one eye shining and the other one dangling from the socket was when you decided the old tom had to retire.

We took him to the vet, where the blinded eye was reinserted in the socket. You had him neutered. And he moved into the basement/garage.

"Satan's downstairs," you'd joke, after dubbing him with that devilish name.

When the winter came and it got cold down there, he moved upstairs into the house, where he enjoyed comfortable retirement, well into his 20s, by the vet's estimate.

You remember when the vet said he had cancer and had to be put to sleep?

As it was becoming my custom, I went with you to the vet, after some tests showed a bulge inside his system to be cancerous. There was no doubt he had to be put down, the vet insisted. I told you I'd hold him while the vet injected him. I would love him and say goodbye as he went to sleep.

Then we asked the vet if he was sure it needed to be done? After all, the old black devil looked pretty good. Maybe we could take him home and bring him back when the cancer got too much.

He lived at least another 10 years. Of course, after the cancer scare, the basement never was home for him again. Mostly he spent his time sunning himself in your front room, perfectly content.

Then there was Sly. One day while I was at your house, visiting as I did most weekends during my first years at the newspaper in Clarksville, you came home with a tiny, barely weaned kitten, covered with oil. He had been in the middle of the road, so you stopped and tried to catch him. Then a truck driver stopped, too. The kitten ran beneath the truck and the truck driver crawled beneath it from one end while you went from the other end and caught him.

To look at you now, it's hard to imagine you crawling beneath a semi-trailer on a heavily trafficked industrial road on a rainy day.

Sly became my cat. He always was wild. A one-man cat, although he could put up with you.

I came to live with you and Dad, seeking a refuge from the storms of life, and Sly came home too. So did Flapjacks and Duke, the dogs.

We'll get back to them.

First I need to talk about Ralph.

He was a cat who looked just like Sly, except he was meek and mild. You found him and decided I needed another cat, so you and Eric brought him up to me in Clarksville. Sly almost killed Ralph, so we decided it would be better if Eric kept Ralph. Eric at the time was living with you, and the five dogs and three cats.

On weekends when I'd come home, there'd be four cats.

CHAPTER SEVENTEEN

The best mom a kid could have

Getting ahead of myself here, some. It's not all about animals, of course.

I remember the fun we used to have at Sylvan Lake, where Marc and Jeff — your brother Joe's sons — often visited, especially during the summers.

Yep, Joe. My uncle.

My son's name is Joe. Boy does he love you. Remember when he first saw you? The day before, he'd flown, screaming, halfway around the world from Romania, where he'd spent three years in an orphanage.

He was afraid of everything. Yet, when he saw you, he sat right down on the window sill next to the bed and smiled at you; called you "Nonny."

Anyway, Uncle Joe and his wife Florence and Grandma and Grandpa Champ would go out to Arizona in the summer in the attempt to help Uncle Joe live longer. He died of the same disease you've been fighting so long...his fueled more quickly by a flame thrower in the Battle of the Bulge and spurred on by cigarettes.

I have so many memories of Uncle Joe. Even though he died in 1957, when I was 6, I remember his smile, his charm, his quick wit and his warm embrace. Even as a little kid, I knew he was sick. But I didn't really understand.

That "understanding" came in one stark tableau that still is fresh in my mind more than 40 years later. It was Thanksgiving Day and we were gathered at Grandma and Grandpa Champ's little home in the hollow at Walnut Lake, Michigan.

I went down the short hall, probably drawn by a strange noise, and saw Grandpa working hard on the oxygen pump, trying to fill his son's lungs with life. At least for a while.

The summers, when Marc and Jeff would come to visit us, often were spent by and in the waters of Sylvan Lake.

We'd go for long walks in the evening. And if we got warm, you'd just stop at the beach and tell us to strip down to our underwear and we'd all go into the water and splash and laugh. You were the best Mom a kid could have.

Remember when I took this girl, Debbie something, to see "Blazing Saddles?" There was a raging thunderstorm outside. When the movie ended, there was this baby sparrow hopping on the sidewalk near the shrubbery outside the theater. I picked up the little bird, had the girl hold it, and we drove it to the house.

You and Dad took the bird from me and we put it in a cage that you kept for injured birds. Often you'd take them to the vet or the wildlife rehab refuge.

We tried to save that bird, but a few days later it died. I buried it in a soap box out behind your house. We've buried all kinds of toads, turtles, birds and squirrels out there.

One bird you rescued was a sparrow with a deformed left foot. He couldn't perch or hop around adequately to feed himself. The veterinarian said there was no way he'd live. He did live for about 10 years in a big cage you had by the window in your guest bedroom. Every morning the house was alive with that bird's singing. His name was simply Bird.

On nice days, you'd take the cage outside and hang it on the eaves over the patio. One day, Bird got the cage opened. And he flew away.

You were crushed. You said it was likely the way God planned it...that you'd given the animal a life and now he was gone. But he'd never make it on his own. Not with only one foot.

You stood up at the edge of the woods and called "Bird...Bird...Bird..." even as your lungs were faltering in those days. And this bird came out of the woods and landed on your shoulder. He stayed there as you walked back to the house.

You cried when he died, years later, and you always missed him; his morning songs and his loyalty to you. You gave him life, where he would look out the window and see the world.

At times, you'd let him out of the cage and allow him to fly around the house, until he got too old or perhaps too blind. He began to crash into things, stunning himself, as he tried to land or negotiate a doorway.

A big reason I fell in love with Suzanne was that she shares your compassion for animals. We have often rescued frogs, turtles, rabbits from the roadway.

When I first met her, Suzanne had an old German shepherd named Pepper. She said Pepper wouldn't take to me, because she was overly protective. After all, Pepper had been trained to protect Suzanne back when she was wandering the roads of rural Arkansas as a police reporter.

It didn't take long for that dog to love me. She lapped at my ears and sat in my lap. When she got older and I was visiting Suzanne, while we were engaged, I would take Pepper for long walks in the little town of Sweetwater where Suzanne was managing editor of the local newspaper.

But Pepper's health began to fail. She had tumors on her organs and they were not operable.

I sat down with Pepper one night and told her that if she could hang on that I would appreciate it. I said I was going to marry her momma, but it would be a few months. Pepper needed to take care of Suzanne until I was able to take over for her. That old dog lived up to her part of the deal. She lived about eight months after Suzanne and I married. Again, for probably the 10th time in my life, I had to carry an animal I loved into the vet clinic so it could be put to sleep.

We've had a lot of animals.

The last time you were in the hospital for so long...well, that was when Dad and I had to have Flapjacks put to sleep.

Suzanne and I had been going by your house to take care of him while you were in your fight out here at the hospital, with Dad, more often than not, sleeping in the recliner by your bed. But Flap was failing.

You remember how Flap came into your house?

When I came home to stay with you and Dad during the end of my first marriage, Flap came with me. And Duke. And I had Sly.

I'd moved home as divorce loomed. I had my three animals and my record albums.

Duke was a golden retriever. Flap was a mixed-breed mutt, the kind you'd call a "Heinz 57" for all the varieties of bloodlines.

Flap came to me via my newspaper stint in Clarksville. It was late at night and I was leaving work in downtown Clarksville. My old Duster, the first new car I ever owned, was parked about three blocks from the newspaper building, over behind the post office. It was about 2 a.m.

Earlier in the evening I'd spoken with you. Storm had been put to sleep that day, another cancer victim. Dad was heartbroken.

And there was this scroungy mutt, pushing and shoving on the front door of the old Royal York Hotel, a refuge for lovable losers and no-account boozers. It was a place where I found so many true friends. Like Skipper. Okey "Skipper" Stepp was the guy who looked like Popeye and told me stories of his life as a Merchant Marine and as a carny.

He's the one who told me about watching the Japanese planes fly past his Pearl Harbor-area apartment on Dec. 7, 1941. Later he had a ship shot out from beneath him in the North Atlantic. And he served spaghetti to Al Capone in Chicago.

Skipper became such a dear friend, someone I took around town, to my house, even on short road trips, partly because of you. I learned not to look down on the less-fortunate. I loved old Skipper. He and I spent a lot of time sitting on the bus bench in front of the flophouse that was the Royal York back in those days.

Fact is, the first time I met Skipper he was sitting on the bench in front of the hotel. We drank coffee. Several times I wrote about him, beginning with the ungrammatical phrase: "Me and old Skipper sat on a bench. It was hot. Boy was it hot."

When he died a few years ago, I wrote a column about him using those same words to say goodbye to him.

Anyway Skipper was not in the hotel any more when that dog was scratching at the front door. Skipper was in a nursing home by then. He died in that nursing home. When I went to tell him I was getting divorced and leaving

Clarksville, he said "Good. I'll miss you. But you need to find someone to make you happy."

The guy who lived a great life of adventure on the seven seas or just a great life of imagination in Clarksville — it didn't matter to me either way — donated his arthritis gnarled body to medical research.

The last night he lived in that hotel was a New Year's. I can't remember which year it was. But I went up to his $5 a night concrete cubicle and helped him pack. There were Zane Grey Westerns and Louis L'Amour books that we jammed in boxes. The radio blared Rick Nelson's "Travelin' Man" as we finished packing. "I'm a travelin' man and I made a lot of stops. All over this world..." is a part of the song lyric. The song ended and the disc jockey said that Nelson and his band had died in a plane crash.

Anyway, my old buddy, Skipper, the travelin' man — if you believed all of his tales or if you just loved him — wasn't there when the dog was scratching at the Royal York door.

But there were several other old fellas I'd befriended in there. They called Skipper "Red" by the way, because he used to be red-headed. Like their buddy, they were Western fans. And on that night, they were watching old cowboy movies on the television in the Royal York lobby.

One fellow, can't think of his name now, once told me from his frail shell that when he was younger "I was so tough my spit would bounce." He was there that night.

The dog wanted to get out of the cool night air and into the lobby. I went into the lobby and asked if anyone owned that dog. They all looked at the door.

Nope, I was told. "You better take him, Tim," said one guy who I remember went by the name "Johnson." First name? Last name? I don't remember. Just "Johnson."

But in the middle of some difficult times, I really didn't want to take a dog home with me. Yet, he followed me into the night. I tried to duck him by walking through the post office, coming out a door a half-block away from where I entered. The mutt was waiting for me at that door.

Then I tried to ditch him when I got into my car. He circled it, howling.

Finally, I got out onto the main street and began cruising home. I looked in my rearview mirror and there was the dog running as fast as he could after the car, down the middle of the avenue.

I stopped, opened up the passenger door, and he jumped right in.

I named him Flapjacks, after the character I'd played in a little movie some friends and I made for charity: "Flapjacks: The Motion Picture."

CHAPTER EIGHTEEN

A little dance at the world premiere

You and Dad and some of your friends came up to Clarksville to see that film, which was our sort of version of The Beatles' "A Hard Day's Night" and "Help!" dosed with the Monkees, social satire and well, just plain old craziness.

That's another story, another day. I do remember you being proud to be there at the theater. You knew, if no one else did, that a big part of the reason for the movie was as a tool for me to cope with my personal and professional demons.

Among the most vivid recollections of the "world premiere" night was of you and Dad dancing on the sidewalk, beneath the marquee, while the Fort Campbell 101st Airborne Jazz Band performed.

Perhaps I can get back to more on this later. If not, well, you know the story and how it comes out.

CHAPTER NINETEEN

Ol' Buddy, Ol' Pal

Anyway, it was obvious from the day I found the dog that his name had to be Flapjacks, Flap for short.

He was shaggy and loving and perhaps a bit confused, kind of like the title character in the movie and kind of like the guy who played that title character.

Later I inherited a golden retriever named Duke. The two dogs were good pals, for the most part. But when my first marriage ended and I came home to your house with the two dogs, something had snapped inside Duke.

The vet thought maybe he had a brain tumor. I was never sure. I don't know. Maybe I didn't spend enough time with him. He was a beauty and he loved me and Dad. He was gentle around people in general. Yet, he had turned vicious to his "best friend" attacking and trying to kill Flap at every opportunity.

You and I took Duke to behavior specialists, who all but said there was nothing that could be done to help him.

Dad helped me when we had to have Duke put to sleep. Duke loved Dad. And Dad loved him, I suppose because the dog reminded him of Storm. Course, Dad has a pretty big heart when it comes to animals, too.

Soon after we put Duke to sleep, the dog whose name

was Flapjacks began to curry favor with Dad, jumping in his lap and watching TV at night. I was working nights in Clarksville, about 60 miles away, gone from your house from about noon until 2 or 3 a.m.

I knew that when I got back on my feet and moved, the dog would not be going with me. Dad even dropped the "s" off the dog's name. He became "Flapjack."

Dad loved Flapjack and had him for another 12 years. Finally, on your last hospital stay in the spring, at least the last one you came home from, Flap began to fail miserably.

He couldn't make it to the door where he had to go out to urinate. His legs would give out or his kidneys would give out. Whatever...he was miserable. Deep inside those dark eyes there was sadness. Of course, there was also confusion. He'd always made it to the door, never had an accident, even after I took him in from the wild, years and years before.

And now his old body was betraying him.

I guess that happens, doesn't it?

He really was a great dog. I know, you thought he was a stupid fellow. But you loved him. We all loved Flapjack. Course, I loved Flapjacks.

Suzanne and I have accumulated our own set of strays.

First there was the dog Suzanne thought was a pot-bellied pig on that morning as she drove to work. The animal was obviously injured, crawling across Nolensville Road and then trying to get up on the curb, unsuccessfully.

In the darkness, Suzanne stopped at the roadside of the four-lane highway and picked up the bloody animal. It wasn't a pig. It was a tiny puppy, chocolate brown.

She took it to the vet to check out and repair. The animal had some broken bones and an injured eye socket and sinuses. He'd be okay if we wanted to take care of him.

We did. The vet said he was a chocolate lab mix of some sort and would be about 55 pounds or so.

Buddy now weighs 130 pounds and turns out he's a German shepherd, chocolate lab mix. A great, big old house dog.

One afternoon shortly after we adopted him, I took Buddy out on his leash in the front yard and he stiffened. The little brown pup was looking at a pink kitten sprawled in the middle of the lawn. I figured the cat belonged to someone, so I pulled Buddy back into the house.

Later that night, I spied the kitten in a shrub, nesting like some sort of tiger. I put food out on the porch next to the shrub. That night we heard the screeching of cats in the darkness. And a fearful mewing.

I pulled on my robe and went outside. The shrub was being attacked by a big, gray cat. The little pink kitten was clinging high in the branches of the cedar, too high for the heavier animal to reach. I grabbed a chunk of mulch to throw at the larger cat.

And as the story goes, after a trip to the vet to be treated for fleas and worms and get his shots, the pink kitten joined our growing household. And the little kitten was actually six months old, dwarfed because of lack of food, the vet guessed.

That little pink, dwarf cat soon was running around our house. He was too small to contain. Tried locking him in the bathroom during the day when we were at work, but he kept climbing under the door. He and the dog would play all day. We named him "Pal."

You thought that was cute. We had a big, brown dog named Buddy and a fattening kitten name Pal.

It was from that great movie we talked about before: "It's a Wonderful Life." George Bailey is talking to Ernie, the cab driver. And he called him "Ol' buddy, ol' pal."

You remember when Suzanne and I bought the house we have on Rochelle Drive in Nashville?

On moving day, you — your health already failing pretty rapidly — couldn't help with the actual moving. But you were able to watch Buddy and Pal.

By the end of the day, you were glad we came to get Buddy. "He's a sweet dog, but he's crazy. I guess that's what they always say: an animal takes on the personality of its master." You looked at me and laughed. I miss that laugh. You haven't had much to laugh about in a long time.

CHAPTER TWENTY

More fried than frazzled

It wasn't long after we moved into the house that Suzanne and I began to try to have a family.

"I always feel sorry for people who don't have children," you would say. "They never will know what life is really about. Children bring you a lot of heartache. But they bring you oh, so much more joy. You've brought me both, son. And I love you so much."

Anyway, Suzanne and I went through all the fertility treatments and tests. We took the medicines. She had surgery. We both went through a host of humiliating procedures. Still we pursued the treatments, the pills, used the thermometers and the cups.

And then we saw the television broadcast.

The Communist Bloc was falling across Eastern Europe. And in one primitive country, Romania, there were orphans stockpiled in institutions all over the country.

Those eyes. Deep brown. Sad.

Babies in cribs.

No parents.

No hope.

The former dictator had ordered that fertile women give birth to at least five children and the fifth one was to be turned over to the state as part of a homegrown work force. So birth control was not allowed.

Even after the dictator was killed, the revolution of freedom a success, the poor peasants who made up most of the country did not practice birth control. Babies continued to be stockpiled in orphanages.

As it became increasingly apparent that Suzanne and I weren't going to have children of our own, as least the old-fashioned way, we began to investigate how to take one of these children into our home. Once we located the adoption agency, we went out to their offices and watched more films about those babies, stuck in their cribs until they are 3.

I will never forget the look on your face when Suzanne and I told you we were going to try to bring home one of these abandoned children.

"You'll never regret it," you said.

And you wept joyfully.

It took a long time to get Emily.

There is so much paperwork, so much expense, so much gnawing of fingernails involved with overseas adoption. All we told Small World — the adoption agency — was that we wanted a baby of either sex, as healthy as possible, 2 years old or younger.

You could be as specific as you wanted to be. We have friends who adopted infants. But the less specific the better for speeding up the process.

At the same time as Suzanne and I worked painstakingly through the adoption process, you and Dad were getting ready to celebrate 50 years of marriage. It was probably a blessing that the two happened at about the same time, because we launched into the preparations for your Golden Anniversary celebration. It kept us all from getting too worried about the long wait for our baby.

For your big party, we had enlargements of photos from your memory books blown up.

Suzanne had painted scores of frames gold. We had mementoes of your lives together.

There were toasts and laughs.

And while you relished the party, or at least relished what was being celebrated, the wear and tear that life was taking on you showed. You fought to stay at the party as long as possible. But then you literally ran out of gas. You needed to get home, off the portable oxygen machine and plugged into the big, humidified oxygen tank.

One thing that Suzanne and I had joked about while the party was being planned was that if the adoption agency called the week before and said we needed to get to Romania, you guys were on your own. You even laughed about that, but said, yep, that's the way it would have to be. Well, the anniversary party was on Saturday. On Monday afternoon, the adoption agency called Suzanne at her office and me at mine. They had a 22-month-old girl in Romania, in an orphanage in Arad, if we were interested. They wanted us to come out to the agency and look at the little girl's picture.

We met there about a half-hour later. And there was this picture of this curly-headed little darling. Her name was Mariana.

"Can you be in Bucharest in three weeks?" the agency director asked us.

The timetable for us getting there, for retrieving Mariana, and for getting home had already been worked out. The agency director somehow knew that we were going to take her and had begun the proceedings in Romania to legally make her ours.

"When we said we might have to leave the anniversary celebration to get Emily, we almost were right," Suzanne joked as we got into the cars to drive home.

Three weeks later we were in Bucharest. And 12 days after that, Mom, you were waiting in the concourse of Nashville International Airport to welcome your newest granddaughter.

You were in a wheelchair. It was almost 90 degrees out even in this late evening. But you had to see her. Emily Mariana Ghianni, 23 months old, had to be greeted by her Nonna, her Papa and Grandma and Grandpa (Suzanne's folks).

After an all-day series of flights, you told me it looked like I needed a haircut. That was your standard line when it came to trying to joke me.

I'd cut it right now if it would make you feel better. But it won't help, so I'll let it grow.

The trip to get Emily was perhaps the most strenuous part of my entire life. I lost 15 pounds on that trip. I lived on cigarettes and energy bars. Romanian food, for the most part, isn't that good. Although we did have one fine dinner trip in Transylvania, after visiting Dracula's castle.

I was almost 44 when I became a dad. Suzanne's about nine years younger.

But both of us were emotionally and physically wasted, out of it, frazzled, whatever term you want to use, when we got off the plane in Nashville. I can't tell you how hard it is to entertain a child for almost 24 hours of flight and layover time.

Mostly what we did on the plane was play a little game, over and over. Emily would pull the pieces of paper — flight evac plans, puke bags, stuff like that — from the pocket of the seat in front of her. She'd drop it on the floor. Her Daddy would pick it up and put it back in the pocket. She'd laugh. And over and over it went. For hours and hours. The kid drops the paper. The dad picks it up....

Anyway, when we got back to Nashville, you told me I looked pretty much "like crap" or something like that. I can't remember the exact wording.

And your daughter-in-law, you said, looked out of it.

Me, I felt more fried than frazzled. Wasted in the airport in my Hawaiian shirt and jeans.

But both of us, you added, looked like we'd just been through a terribly long and arduous birthing. I think you were proud of yourself for saying that.

You are kind of a smart ass, you know. I can talk to you like that now.

You always did know I talked like that.

Anyway, Suzanne and I went back to our house that night and collapsed in our own bed. The next morning we awoke early to check on our baby who was sleeping quietly between us.

"You know, that really was a long, strange trip," I said, borrowing a phrase from Jerry Garcia. About the only news from the outside world we got when we were in Romania was when they started playing Grateful Dead tunes on the public bus sound system. Jerry Garcia, the American musician, has died, the announcer said as we just kept truckin' along.

Just days back from Romania, we started saving for the next trip. Soon we were filing the first paperwork and paying the first of the $30,000 in fees and expenses that led us to having a son in our house...the little fellow who loves his "Nonny."

Joseph Glen Ghianni.

Named for your brother, at least in part. The name Joseph is in both families. A lot of Josephs.

I kind of wanted to use the name John, after John Lennon, but Suzanne nixed that idea. The youngsters who didn't grow up in the heat of Beatlemania, whose parents didn't buy them that first Beatles single, just don't get it.

The story of Joe is pretty much like that of Emily. It was about two years after we got her that the adoption agency called us to their office. We had asked for a boy or girl, 2½ years old or younger.

The adoption agency had told us it was going to be a while. Adoptions were tightening up in Romania.

But then they called. They had this little boy available. He was just shy of 3 years old. He was supposed to be adopted by another family, but just days short of his rescue, that family had to back out. The agency had one day to place him again with a different family. If that wasn't done, they would lose him to another agency. And at age 3, he would be shuffled from the toddlers' orphanage to one for older boys.

Generally these older boys are the ones who are never adopted. They are the ones who crawl out of the sewers on crisp Bucharest mornings and try to pick your pocket while their sisters try to sell you their bodies.

Sometimes it's vice versa. And, the fact that the boys also are for sale made Bucharest the pedophile vacation destination of choice in Europe.

At the adoption agency, we looked into the eyes of the little boy in the picture as he stood in his crib. We flipped over to the page that had any health information.

"Healthy," it said. "He's a charming character." That was all the information.

"When can we go get him?" we asked the adoption officials.

A few months later we were back in Romania. We got Joe at the orphanage down in the countryside outside Giurgiu. It is a deep-water seaport on the Danube, across the river from Bulgaria and its gray, intimidating nuclear towers.

It's odd to find yourself deep in the heart of what once was the so-called evil empire of Soviet affiliates. There are nuclear towers and dirty ships. And pathetic poverty.

Joey came from an orphanage that was on a bumpy, rural road.

Ox carts carried peasants from sunflower fields to hops fields. Manure punctuated the rutted roadway. The air smelled of dust and rot. Or maybe death.

At night, apparently drunken sailors may have marched down the bumpy road. When we first got Joey, he would swagger like a drunk around the room, hoisting his arm and singing what for all the world had to be drinking songs. "Oh-we-oh Oh! Oh! Oh-we-oh Oh! Oh!" or something in a similar vein. The closer he got to being fed the louder he became, and the faster he marched. Our little drunken sailor calmed down and quieted as soon as the food was placed before him.

A few miles from the orphanage and inside the town, the sewage sometimes dripped from the above-ground pipes and pre-teen castoffs huddled around in the parks, smoking cigarettes, sniffing glue and asking for handouts.

The experience inside Romania was easier the second time, if for no reason than we'd been there before. And in the three years between trips, the West had caught up some. There were fancy Shell super gas station/markets selling American cigarettes and German biscuits. A Pizza Hut was busy in the city of Bucharest. And while the gypsy kings still reigned over the highways, it just somehow seemed less primitive.

When Joe got his physical in Romania, it was in a modern clinic, not the state-run clinic where Emily was tested. When they drew her blood, they just cut a slit in the back of her hand and let the blood drip into a cup placed on the floor. For Joe they used syringes.

On this trip back from Romania with Joe, we had an unscheduled landing somewhere...perhaps Bosnia. I never did figure out what that was all about. But there were soldiers on the runway. It was one of those times when I thought I ought to use the paper bag in the pocket in the seat in front of me.

After we got home this time, we didn't jump to say we were going to get another. For one thing, we already spent $60,000-plus and years of our lives doing this. Another thing, well, I truly was getting too old to qualify for another adoption from Romania.

CHAPTER TWENTY-ONE

An ending worthy of Frank Capra

You weren't at the airport for Joey's arrival.

But the next day we came to see you.

"Why, hello, Joey," you said as the little boy wandered into the room where you were in bed. "I'm your Nonna."

Joey laughed and sat down on the window ledge about two feet from you.

"Nonny. Nonny!" he chirped.

Something about you has set him at ease from the very beginning. Was there a kindly old woman in Giurgiu who befriended him? Did he have contact with older people?

We've been told that his biological mother lived in a one-room shack with no water or electricity and dirt floors. Several other people lived in the house. Perhaps there was a Nonny there that Joey met before his mother realized she couldn't afford to feed him.

I could keep going here, but this pretty much is the end of the story about how you taught me to take in strays. And look where it got me? I have two of the most beautiful kids in the world. I have a wife who not only took in animals and babies, but who took me in as well when I needed to be taken in from the storms of life.

Oh, how I wish I had taken a picture of the last time Joey

was visiting you before you got sick last Sunday. He just wandered right into your bedroom, climbed up on the bed and propped himself on the pillow next to yours.

"Hi Nonny," he said.

Even at your weakest, you just had to laugh.

And Emily — who was there using your swimming pool for her birthday party — just laughed at her brother from the foot of the bed.

Too bad old Flapjacks didn't make it long enough to share that scene. It would have been an almost perfect final scene for this story. You know, the "It's a Wonderful Life" bit where we all gather together in one room and wait for a bell to ring. "Attaboy, Clarence," I would wink at the angel as we all broke into "Auld Lang Syne."

An ending worthy of Frank Capra, of course. But Mom, I keep remembering stuff, so I can't stop yet.

CHAPTER TWENTY-TWO

Confronting mortality

I remember when you had the stroke when I was in high school.

Eric and I were at wrestling practice. When we were done, you were supposed to come and pick us up. Sometimes we caught rides with other guys, sometimes they hitched with us, or with you as the chauffeur.

Anyway, Dad was on the road, in Iowa or Minnesota or California, I can't remember. When I called you from the locker room to say that practice was done and Eric and I would be ready for our ride home in a few minutes, you answered kinda woozily, if that's a word, saying you could come get us, but you'd prefer if we got someone else to give us a ride.

You said the doctor had been there that day and that you had had a stroke.

I have no doubt that you would have come and gotten us, but I hollered out for someone to give us a ride and we were home shortly. You were in bed. The doctor, I can't remember his name anymore. Jewish fella. Nice guy. He was still there. Hold it, it just came to me: Dr. Szyman, I think it was.

He told us you had a busted aneurysm in your brain; that you would be okay, but you needed to stay in bed. And we needed to make sure you took your medicine.

It was a prescription of injections to be given in your bottom. Neither Eric nor I felt like this was something we wanted to do. Fortunately, you and the doctor said you could do it yourself.

"But you better call your father," the doctor told me. We put out calls to all of his business associates from the phone list he kept in his downstairs office. We sat there and waited for him to call back.

It sticks in my mind that Eric and I watched a Jackie Gleason movie called "Papa's Delicate Condition" — kind of appropriate in a backwards sort of way — while we waited for the call.

Dad finally did call and was on the first plane back to O'Hare. I picked him up in the middle of the night. Any excuse to goose your '65 Falcon Futura to the 80-90 mile per hour range, slowing only to throw loose change in the basket at the toll booths.

I really liked that car. It eventually became mine, and I used it to drive back and forth to college. I also used the Falcon on my trip to discover America after graduating from college.

After that stroke, you recovered quickly, you were okay. But I'd never seen you weak before. And in a lot of ways, this was the first time I confronted my mom's mortality.

As it turns out, I confronted your mortality for most of the last hard years of your life.

When the doc told us how sick you had been, I knew that you could have died.

"What if we'd come home and found Mom dead?" I asked Eric.

He shrugged. You know him.

And he had a nervous laugh.

But you know there have been countless times in recent years when I raced to your house or to the hospital and wondered basically the same thing. Sometimes you'd be sleeping and I'd listen closely for breath, touch your wrist for pulse.

"What if I get there and Mom's dead?"

I guess you will be pretty soon.

CHAPTER TWENTY-THREE

'We are the Dingbats'

You remember when I played football in high school, even though you didn't think I ought to?

Of course, you were right. I wasn't very good at it. And I didn't like it. It was hours and hours of drudgery in the hot August sun for two-a-days, only to be a blocking dummy during weekday practice.

I did this because Eric did it before me. He was good. But he also had the advantage of having Dad to coach him all his life. I never showed any interest, so Dad didn't coach me.

Even back in Grand Rapids, when Eric was playing Rocket football, Dad was the coach of the team. They played night games over at the old South High School stadium.

Jimmy Haan and I chose to be water boys instead.

And that was fun, hoping those bigger boys were thirsty.

Anyway, we moved from Grand Rapids to Deerfield, and by the time I got to high school in that suburban Chicago town, Eric already was a starting offensive lineman. I didn't play football at first. I did wrestle, but that was mainly to get into shape and apparently to help me fuel some habits.

But this time we're talking football.

The family tradition.

And I wasn't buying in.

I was content to work at the school newspaper, get my share of A's without really trying very hard, listen to The Beatles and The Stones, go to the movies on the weekend, sometimes staying twice through double features, especially if they were James Bond movies.

Coaches and teachers were asking when I was gonna play football like my brother.

Finally in my junior year, I relented. I went out for the team. I was no good. About the only thing I accomplished that year came in two-a-days.

That was back in the pre-Gatorade days, when men were men and no one drank liquids during practice. It was considered "sissy" to be thirsty and drink. Sweat it out. Don't look for something to drink.

One afternoon, right as practice ended, everything all of the sudden turned bleary. I couldn't talk to the coach to say what was wrong. I couldn't hear anything. The other players could see something was horribly wrong with me. But they knew the rules. We all had to get back to the locker room in just five minutes or we would be back out on the field running wind sprints.

As I ran, I began to weave, stumble, fall to the ground. The other guys worried about me. They also didn't want to do wind sprints when it was 90 out. So they picked me up by the shoulder pads. I moved my legs, but I don't think I touched the ground. Maybe they carried me. Maybe my feet did touch. I was so sick, I didn't know what I was doing.

When they sat me down outside the locker room to take off my cleats, I just fell back. The next thing I knew I was lying on my back in the shower room, cold water pounding on me. One of the former players, a guy who was working out with the team to get ready for his freshman year at

Nebraska, held onto my head.

An ambulance was on the way. I faded in and out. I remember crying that "I don't want to die" and then falling into the wall of lockers.

I was put into the ambulance and hauled to the hospital. I woke up in downtown Highland Park, on that long hill where traffic always stacked up. Dad was right behind us in the car.

The ambulance was running lights and siren and blew through the intersection.

"I've always wanted to do that," I said, realizing no one could hear me because I was wearing an oxygen mask. One of the attendants did give me sort of a thumbs-up after noting that I was awake.

When they rolled me into the ER, they continued to work on me, first with IVs and ice packs and cold water treatments, then they had me drinking orange juice and eating crackers.

"How are you Timmy?" Dad asked as he leaned over the foot of my gurney.

It was at that precise moment that the orange juice hit bottom and it wasn't going to stay there, I lurched up from my prone position and projectile vomited orange juice and crackers all over Dad.

To his credit, he just shrugged. A guy who shot it out with Japanese snipers in the Philippines wasn't going to be sickened by a little puke.

Mom, you got there, and Dad went home briefly to change clothes.

It was a lot of hours and a lot of hydration before I left the hospital. And despite your pleas, I rejoined the ball team a couple of weeks later. The problem was, and continues to this day, that once you suffer from severe dehydration, heat exhaustion, your body chemistry changes and you always sweat too much.

You probably don't remember this now, but it was at that time that Dr. Szyman began prescribing thyroid and diet pills.

I found that I took a liking to diet pills. They helped me make my weigh-in for wrestling matches, allowed me to keep doing take-downs at practice long after the other guys were drained. I wasn't good... just fast.

Often, particularly as the next football season rolled around, I would take an extra couple of pills to get the edge. Yeah Mom, you know me and "addictive personality." I didn't know anything was wrong with what I was doing. I do know it made me run faster and hit harder.

Suddenly I was growing. I started my senior season at something like 5-foot-6 and by late October I was 6-foot-2, well on the way to the 6-3 that I eventually reached.

Anyway, about halfway through the season, I was in practice, just a normal JayVee player, having fun during our scrappy little games no one attended during the week, in which I was starting defensive end.

Those were fun games. No pressure. The good players all had the day off from practice. Probably sucking on chili dogs outside the Tastee Freez with the cheerleaders.

It turned out that as I grew, I was getting better and better. And faster. I wasn't good enough to play varsity, but I was getting quite a reputation among the rag-taggers of the Central Suburban League JayVee squads. I was fast-roaming, could read the offense and I loved to hit.

Of course, when it came time for practice with the varsity, we were supposed to be chewed up by the bigger and better. The elite.

"We are the Dingbats.

"Mighty, mighty Dingbats.

"Everywhere we go,

"People want to know.

"Who we are.

"So we tell them.

"We are the Dingbats."

In the JayVee world, our coach called us "Dingbats." He had little respect for us, so to irritate him sometimes, I led the fellas on the scrub squad through our own "proud-to-be-Dingbats" version of the "Warrior Victory" song. There were smiles.

Then we all hunkered down and took our duties a little more seriously. Yeah, we were supposed to get the crap kicked out of us by the varsity.

But on tackling and blocking drills, we would cheer for each other. Our kind. Dingbats. The coach didn't like it, but he couldn't very well shoot down the camaraderie of a bunch of mostly undersized, definitely under-skilled guys who never got close to a game jersey. We spent Saturday afternoons in the stands. Heck, some of us even began growing sideburns, definitely team rule violations. But we were the Dingbats, you see. We really didn't matter.

Anyway, this sets up what became my final act in football.

The coach wanted us to run a tackling drill. The quarterback was to pitch to the tailback, who was supposed to run at, and over, each of us on the Dingbat squad.

This was not going to happen on this day. No way.

Anyway, Eddie Mount was given the ball. He tucked it and ran right at me. I sprang from my stance and planted my helmet squarely beneath his sternum. He was down.

The coach hollered at Mount to get up and get past me.

Time and again the best running back on our team came at me. And time and again, I planted him on his back. He was angry. I was enjoying every minute of it. Varsity and Dingbat players all came over to watch, forming a gauntlet between which Eddie and I battled in the dust.

They all were hollering for me. No one felt sorry for Eddie as he, time after time, got up and rehitched his shoulder pads, adjusted his helmet and waited for the pitch from the QB.

Finally, in order to avoid more punishment to his midsection, Eddie lowered his helmet just before impact. The webbing inside mine broke during that helmet-to-helmet crash. I didn't find that out until later. In fact, I didn't realize much at the time.

I just remember coming to consciousness as the ambulance crossed the little bridge over the stream that separated the practice fields from the high school. I looked over to see my helmet, all the webbing and ropes red from blood, laying beside me.

I had a lot of stitches at the top of my head. Minor concussion. I had to miss a couple of days of school. I found out later that Eddie Mount's spleen had been ruptured on that day and he missed a game or two. But he had a pretty good season anyway.

The problem this time was that the coaches were impressed. Finally, they had their mean Ghianni fighting machine. No longer, in their minds at least, was I a Dingbat, even though I actually was quite proud to be a leader of that band of outcasts. When I returned to practice a week or so later, my locker had been moved. I was in the plush varsity locker room. My name was on my locker. My helmet was all cleaned up and ready to play.

"You are a Man now," said the coach. "You are mean."

I thought about that for a couple of days. Our homecoming game was that Saturday. I can't remember who we were playing. And, no, this isn't a movie and I didn't make the starting lineup. But I did dress out. And my buddies all sat up in the stands. I was down on the bench in the red and gray colors and the scarred helmet because I was "mean."

Early in the game, one of our guards went down with a knee injury. The coach didn't waste a second. He called out to me. "You earned it, Dingbat. Get your ass in there and kill them. You are a Brahma Bull."

You were in the stands, Mom, so you know what happened next. I was horrible on that next series of plays. I blew my assignments. I couldn't hit anybody, hard or otherwise. What you don't know...what I've never told anybody before is that I took a dive. I didn't like being thought of as mean. I didn't like that I had to barbarically pound some poor tailback into the hospital in order to play the game.

Yeah, on the JayVee field, I was plenty good enough and I was big and fast... faster than most of the running backs and wideouts even on the varsity. But those were games that no one cared about. The head coach never attended, never applauded you for being mean.

Well, on that series of defensive plays, my only real varsity experience, I simply and willfully took a dive. I played poorly on purpose. I decided I didn't like being mean. "Screw you coach," I muttered as I ran to the sidelines after an opposing player cleared my spot in the line to score a touchdown.

The head coach, who played his college ball with Dick Butkus, gave me a dirty look. He never put me back in the ballgame. I kept my named locker, but I never got back in a varsity game. I spent Mondays after school playing the Dingbat way.

At the end of the season, a snowy day at New Trier, the coach walked through the locker room, shaking hands with everybody or offering encouraging words to others.

He looked down his crooked nose at me as I pulled my cleats off for the last time. "I thought you were mean, Ghianni."

"I'm not," I said. "And you are an asshole."

You like that one, Mom. I can see you trying to smile. I'm going to go get a cup of coffee and come back in. I've got some more things to talk about if you aren't going anywhere soon.

You are smiling at that, too, Mom.

Chapter Twenty-Four

A shoebox full of toads

"Hi Mom, it's Tim."

I'm back. I had a couple of cups of coffee.

I was here a few minutes ago, but the therapist was working with you.

So I went back out and had more coffee. Snuck out and had a cigarette, too, Mom.

Sorry I never quit them while you were healthy.

Padre saw me out there and said if smoking was the worst thing I did, I was okay.

My thing isn't that I think smoking is bad. It's just that you've asked me to quit so many times. "You don't want your lungs to end up like mine, Timothy," you'd say. Of course, yours wasn't from smoking. And I've been smoking for something like 30 years.

I started smoking cigars after school back in Deerfield. I'd drive the Falcon out to the Highland Park and park on the bluff overlooking the beach. Probably big houses there now. Back then it was just a turnaround at a dead end. I'd grab my cigars out of the glove box and fire one up from the cigarette lighter. Then I'd amble down the hill and wander on the beach.

I did that almost every day when I was a senior. After I

quit athletics. After you pretty much gave me the car to drive all the time.

Of course, you knew I was smoking cigars.

That didn't really bother you. First of all, that was back in the days before it became un-politically correct — is that the right way to say that? — to smoke. Come to think of it, cigars are kind of "in" nowadays. How could it be okay to inhale one of those big brown rolled leafs and not okay to smoke a cigarette? It's all trends, of course. I was always kind of anti-trend in regard to a lot of things, I guess.

But back to smoking cigars. I learned to smoke cigars by watching your dad, Grandpa Champ, during glorious days when I was a kid and we'd spend part of the summer and a lot of the holidays at Grandma and Grandpa's little house at the edge of the bog at Walnut Lake.

That was great for a kid to have grandparents who lived by the lake.

You remember all the little toads they used to have by their house?

One year, I brought a shoebox filled with them back to our house in Chicago and let them go in the garden. There were always those tiny toads from then on. Probably their descendants are eating the bugs in the gardens there behind the house in Deerfield to this day. Unless they've made it into a shopping mall.

Anyway, I could go on and on about the summers at Walnut Lake. About the way the dirt roads were sprayed with oil to keep the dust down and the way that oil would coat our bare feet when we crossed the roads on the way to the lake.

I could go on about those holidays.

Several things stay in my mind forever.

First of all, Grandpa always had a cigar or a pipe going. I

loved the smells. I took up smoking probably because of those smells. And the fact I loved Grandpa like a pal.

Later on in his life, when he came to live with you and Dad for a while after Grandma died, he and I shared many a good pipe full of tobacco or a cigar or two while we played cribbage.

I still have his cribbage board someplace in my junk. I also have his shaving razor, the one he carried with him back during his cowboy and wheat-threshing times in the dying days of the old and still Wild, Wild West.

He told me a lot of stories about those days, about how he would leave his home in Clayville and get on the road again.

CHAPTER TWENTY-FIVE

Beautiful smell of fried perch

Grandpa Champ first left his home at age 16 — after working a few years as a blacksmith for his dad — in early summer.

He'd take the long train ride to Chicago, where he sometimes worked in beer parlors or delivered beer kegs, whatever jobs he could muster to make a few bucks. He also loved the ballgames at Wrigley Field, the Cubbies.

They say back in Clayville, that town at the foot of what I think they called "Little Mountain" in Upstate New York, he was the best ballplayer ever to take the diamond.

His massive, arthritis-gnarled hands still could grip the baseball even when nothing else seemed to fit adequately during his final days. Your hands are lot like his, aren't they, Mom?

Anyway, after a time enjoying and working in the Windy City, Grandpa and some friends would get on trains that were bound for the still Wild West, the far Northwest at that. They'd travel all the way to Vancouver, British Columbia, and the Pacific Northwest of Canada. Then, beginning there in the coldest and shortest summer in North America, he'd begin working the harvest.

He and his buddies would travel with the weather,

working the threshing machines all the way from the Pacific back to Chicago.

They would follow the arrival of autumn and the harvest season, sign on as laborers and work until they gave out. When they couldn't find work on the threshing crews, there always was a bit of day labor to be had at farms, ranches along the way.

It was 1910 or so and there was plenty of work to be had as the prairies were being cleared for settlement, as towns sprouted up among the prairie dogs.

And, of course, if a guy got down on his luck, he always could rely on his poker-playing skills. Grandpa was the best card player I ever knew. Even as a little boy, he wouldn't let the other guy win.

While we smoked and played cards in his last days, we also usually split a couple of beers.

I'd come home from Clarksville on weekends, which for me was Sunday and Monday. Every Monday we'd take him to the doctor. He'd had a heart attack after Grandma died and he needed those regular checkups.

I think he was okay with me being his wheelchair driver. A lesser man may have been humiliated by his grandson pushing him around the house and then into the doctor's office. And I think he really enjoyed that I would come down and do it. I think he wouldn't have wanted you to be pushing him around.

Grandpa Champ was a great man.

I didn't see him as a sick old man. He was not crippled in my mind. It was during those times when he was in the wheelchair in your house that Grandpa told me stories about how in Minneapolis and St. Paul, one side of the river was wet, the other dry...alcohol-wise, that is. The young adventurers, these threshermen, would walk at night over a precarious plank bridge to get to the wet side of the Mississippi. It was where all the pleasures were.

Grandpa told me he stayed away from many of those pleasures because someplace along the way, and I can't remember now how this happened, he had fallen in love with Beatrice Conger.

Even when he was reveling in his youth in the bars of the West or during pre-World War I days in Chicago, he always had one thought on his mind, one person who he knew was waiting for him.

"She was a good woman," he told me on more than one occasion. I hear that sentiment echoed from you every time you talk about Dad: "He is a good man," you say.

"She took care of me all those years after my arthritis crippled me," he'd tell me in those months after her death.

And I do recall that back at Walnut Lake, it wasn't unusual to hear Grandpa yell "Bea! Bea! Bea!" and no matter where she was, Grandma would some charging back to take care of him. Whether it was to fix another plate of the scrambled eggs and kippers he liked so much or to get him a beer, she was always there. And there was always love in her eyes.

I've gotta tell you something about Grandma. You know a lot of my political leanings were because of her. She was the world's greatest socialist, you know.

She would irritate Grandpa when she'd talk about the way "the Negroes" had been mistreated. She didn't called them "Coloreds," which was the accepted terminology in many quarters back then.

I guess my greatest first-hand lesson in the way she felt everyone was equal — that everyone deserved a chance, no one should be looked down upon — came when I was maybe 11 or so and bound for a Greyhound bus ride from Detroit back to Chicago.

Eric and I had been visiting our grandparents in Michigan and it was time for the two of us to head home via the bus. Grandpa drove us to the station and Grandma came along to make sure Brother and I got on board safely. When we got to the bus station in downtown Detroit the tickets for the Chicago bus were sold out.

Seems more than one busload of Freedom Riders, black demonstrators, whatever they were called back in those early days of the Civil Rights struggle, were bound for Chicago.

I don't know where they were going from there, whether it was down into the South to help Doctor King or whether it was for demonstrations in Chicago. I just remember that being a youngster confronting a busload of black people made me feel a bit uneasy at first. Even Eric, who was to travel on the same bus, seemed a little uneasy. But Grandma just smiled. She was able to buy the tickets. Then she talked with some of the folks and told them to look out for us.

She talked to them about their struggle and why she was on their side, why she hoped they succeeded. She talked to them as the equals she knew they were.

The black people on the bus went out of their way to make us feel comfortable all the way back to Chicago and stayed with us in the bus station there until you and Dad got there to pick us up.

I can only imagine that if she was a few decades younger, Grandma would have been swaying back and forth with a lighted candle singing "We Shall Overcome" with Martin and chanting "All We Are Saying is Give Peace a Chance" with my beloved pal John Lennon at political demonstrations. As for Grandpa, well, he was a bit more conservative, soft-hearted and hardly a bigot. But he enjoyed making fun of Grandma's passions for those less-fortunate.

I always feel bad that when Grandma died of leukemia up in Detroit, I wasn't there. But I'll always remember how well she baited the hook when she took me out fishing at 5 in the morning on Walnut Lake. She'd wear a big straw hat and pull on the oars of a borrowed boat and we'd put nightcrawlers onto the hooks of the bamboo cane poles. We'd spent the night before, per her instructions, digging for those worms in the soil near her tomato, cucumbers and rhubarb garden.

We'd almost always come back with a mess of trout, bass, perch and sunfish, even sometimes a bullhead or two.

Grandpa would help us clean them on the stump back by the trash fire at the back of the yard. Perch and sunfish were easy to clean. Scale them, then chop off the head just below the gills. Finally, then slice the knife up the gut and scrape out the innards.

But bullfish, small catfish kin, had to be skinned. Grandpa would do that after driving a nail through their heads to secure them to the stump. Took the fight out of them, too, I suppose. It sure would have taken the fight out of me, you know.

We'd bury the innards at the edge of the bog. And later it was a good place to come looking for bait.

That house smelled of fried perch almost all the time we were visiting there in the summer.

Oh, I could go on and on, here. But you and I, we've been through this before.

CHAPTER TWENTY-SIX

Walnut Lake

You remember your father and how he could float like a whale out there in the lake? Even though he was pretty crippled up and couldn't sit for long in a single place, at least not on a hard chair or in a boat, he could get in the water.

He would just roll over onto his back and float. He'd go to sleep floating out in the middle of the lake.

When I became a good enough swimmer as a small boy, I would swim out there and wake him...ask him if I could climb on his belly. I remember lying there, on top of this big, big man. He was sleeping and I was smiling. And the cool waters of Walnut Lake made this just about the perfect summer memory.

When Grandpa died, Eric called me at my office in Clarksville. I cried my way through a story I had to get done on deadline. That's the way I was raised. Probably the way George Champ would have done it. Business comes first. It was the life I had chosen.

And then I got in the old '65 Falcon and drove to your house.

You and Aunt Rita had discovered him that morning when he didn't get up for breakfast. He'd never miss his heavily peppered scrambled eggs, after all.

His body was gone from the house when I got there. I couldn't believe he was gone. My friend. The fellow who gave me my mom and my middle name was gone.

I remember that Dad sensed something was wrong, other than the obvious, of course.

"You need to see him?"

I nodded.

We went to the funeral home and for some reason we weren't stopped as we wandered to the embalming room, where Grandpa's mostly naked body lay on a metal table, the veins that had been drained protruding.

"He'll look better soon," the undertaker said as he caught us and escorted us from the room of death.

"I love you, Grandpa," I said, as soon as we got outside and I stared up at the pure blue Nashville skies of the middle 1970s. "I'll miss you."

On the way back to the house, Dad and I talked about the good vacation days at Walnut Lake.

CHAPTER TWENTY-SEVEN

Don't go away

I have a lot of other great vacation memories. Not all of them involved ringworm.

You and Dad would always take us places in the summer. Of course, there was the summer of the visit to Robert E. Lee's dead horse, or whatever that is stuck in my head, way back when I was 3.

We'd go wherever you and Dad had a notion.

We'd go to the Wisconsin Dells.

Or we'd take the Milwaukee Clipper from Muskegon to Milwaukee and drive all the way across the top of the Midwest, tracing the shores of Lake Superior. Whenever I hear that old Gordon Lightfoot song, "The Edmund Fitzgerald" about the freighter lost in the Great Lakes, I think of those wild waters lashing the rocky shores.

From the lake shore, we'd visit the copper mines. We'd eat at a place that had statues of Paul Bunyan and Babe the Blue Ox outside.

We'd visit reservations where we'd see Indian dances and powwows.

Remember parking the car in the dump to watch the bears at night?

I imagine most of those sorts of pleasures are gone now

as theme parks, glitzy resorts and the bed and breakfast gentility take over for the old-fashioned family trek from motel to motel. Don't imagine Upper Peninsula chambers of commerce encourage visitors to go to dumps after dark and sit on their car hoods looking at the marauding bears.

Remember when we went to Wolf Lake Dude Ranch for a week and learned how to ride horses?

Remember the little palomino I was riding got spooked by the older girl who slapped his rump and the little horse tore off in the woods, full gallop, with me holding onto the saddle horn?

The trail boss had to chase me down and rein in the horse. Dad was riding as fast as he could behind me as the other half of the posse.

That girl wasn't allowed to ride any more after that. There was something wrong with her. She was mean. Nuts. Whatever.

I guess it was pretty dangerous. I remember it as fun. I also remember eating beans around the campfire.

I still worry about one summer vacation, though. I think it was at a place called Big Star Lake. You were pregnant and had just begun telling people. You were excited. And up there at the lake, you got sick. We had to leave. Dad had to get you back to Grand Rapids and the doctor.

You lost the baby. It was a little girl, you told us.

I know you were heartbroken.

I've always blamed myself, I don't know why. It was something about how my blood type changed your ability to have a healthy child. I'd go look it up, but there aren't any books in the hospital that I understand. Don't think it would be in those old Peoples and Sports Illustrateds out in the CCU waiting room.

In my nightmares, I see myself pounding you in the stomach. I know I didn't do that. I even asked you once if I did, because those nightmares were so real.

No, you tell me. It's just the positive-negative blood thing, whatever it's called. My blood type was negative. Yours is positive. Or whatever. I can't remember now. Anyway, because of that, it changed stuff inside you that made it improbable for you to have another baby.

You told me that if you had to stop having babies, you were happy that the one you stopped after was me.

Me too, Mom.

Hey Mom. I'm looking at the monitors now. It looks like you are doing a little better. At least now.

Maybe this is helping some. Well, I know it's helping me, anyway.

Nurse is coming in again to change your IV and turn you over. I'm going to go get some more coffee.

I'll see you in a little while. Don't go away.

I've got a few more things to say.

They say I can come back again in about a half-hour. I've probably got time to go grab a smoke.

I was hoping that would bring a little reaction.

Guess you're tired.

I love you, Mom.

CHAPTER TWENTY-EIGHT

Revisiting Flapjacks

"Hi Mom, it's Tim."

I asked the nurse if all this talking I'm doing might be wearing you out. She said it's probably good for you. Mainly, I guess, it's good for me.

I just want you to know that when you leave me, I have mostly good memories.

Hey, I guess now's a good time to revisit that movie: "Flapjacks: The Motion Picture." We talked about it a little bit ago, you know, you dancing beneath the marquee at the world premiere.

You told me my friends and I were crazy. Mostly, of course, you knew I was crazy, and you realized that this movie was my latest way of trying to escape the pressures of a young life that often was taken all-too-seriously.

My friend, Rob Dollar, told me after the night of the premiere, he and I should have simply disappeared into the night, that we never were going to top the legend we'd created.

Well, we didn't disappear. But we did our darnedest to have fun while creating that legend. It was simply, like I said before, sort of "A Hard Day's Night" meets "The Monkees" — with maybe a bit of the Three Stooges thrown in.

We made it to mock the lives of newspapermen and make fun of about everything we could think of. That was back in the Super 8 days, before everybody went video. That would have made it easier, but not as creative, I think.

We shot our little silent movie, fully scripted, and then later added narration and music on a tape we played along with the movie.

Of course, Skipper was in the movie. He was still alive then.

And Tony Durr was in the movie, too, briefly. He was the guy we were trying to find, sort of our version of Monty Python's Holy Grail. The basic plot had Tony disappear from his job as editor and we went off in search of him.

In real life Tony eventually disappeared, some say a suicide. Or at least alone and very sad. But this isn't the time to talk about the death of friends.

We got John Glenn in the movie, simply by running up to him, dodging Secret Service agents, when he was landing in Clarksville for a campaign stop. "I'd like to meet these young guys," he said to the agents who were trying to keep us away. I wedged my body between the open door and the car body, so the agent couldn't slam us out of the way. John Glenn was a nice fellow, though. I think he enjoyed it. Those Mercury astronauts had the Right Stuff, they said in that book. Probably means they were all nuts.

Course, he never was elected president. Probably because he was nice to The News Brothers.

You remember Harold Lynch was in the movie, too? He was the gunslinger in the gunfight, the guy we called "The Stranger." He lost the shootout. A gifted reporter and a nice man, he also later lost a fight to cancer.

Heck we even had Jimmy Stewart in the movie, thanks to

the fact we stole a scene from "The Spirit of St. Louis."

Even when I see him as Lindbergh, I can't help but think of George Bailey, of that building and loan. Luckiest man in Bedford Falls.

Anyway, I can't spend a lot of time going over that movie. I'm sure you've seen it one time too many.

Looking at you now, I can't help but keep smiling by the memory of when you and Dad and all your friends rolled up on Franklin Street in downtown Clarksville to see the movie in the abandoned movie theater we'd reclaimed. It turns out that the old Roxy, which was going to be torn down to make room for a parking lot, was revived by our movie.

We cleaned up the joint, chased off the rats and pigeons, made it look presentable, even had our names in lights on the marquee. Enough of the powers-that-be in Clarksville showed up to stir some interest in keeping the theater. And it wasn't torn down. Now it's a non-profit community theater. Flourishing, too.

Anyway, when you guys rolled up, there was the 101st Band playing beneath your son's name up in lights. I mean, I was Flapjacks.

My buddies and I arrived at the premiere on a fire engine, screaming down the street.

We got them to cooperate, because the funds gathered from ticket sales and concessions went to the Fire Department's victims' relief fund and to other charities.

Anyway, when we jumped from the running boards of the fire engine, there you were, with Dad and your friends. Dancing, arm-in-arm, keeping up with the tempo of the Army band.

My mother enjoying the adventure.

It was like that March 1974 night we snuck in the back

door, the alley door, of the Ryman Auditorium on the last night the Opry was down there before it moved its full-time home out in the suburbs.

I wanted to be there for the final songs, and Johnny Cash, who was your favorite, was going to be there, leading the musical farewell from that stage. "Will the Circle Be Unbroken" they sang.

CHAPTER TWENTY-NINE

'Will The Circle Be Unbroken?'

Well, you know Mom, I've crashed a lot of concerts in my life. One time I got caught when I tried to get into the Beach Boys show. Dennis Wilson and his brothers, Brian and Carl, stood outside the arena when the security guys carted me away. They were laughing. The air smelled kind of sweet. Good vibrations, I guess.

The cops liked me, shared cigarettes with me, enjoyed telling stories to me, so that one ended okay. A little wrist slap and don't do that again sort of thing.

Anyway, of all the shows I used to slip into or try to slip into, my greatest memory of crashing into a show was crashing into the last night of the Opry at the Ryman, with my mom and dad to see Johnny Cash, George Morgan, Mama Maybelle, Dobie Gray, June.

I remember how much you liked Johnny Cash. We used to travel all over the area to catch him when he was performing. You said he had "something special, that magnetism, animal magnetism."

First time I ever saw Carl Perkins, one of my 45 RPM heroes, the rockabilly king who sang "Blue Suede Shoes," it was with you at one of the Johnny Cash shows. Carl was in his band then. You remember I wrote his obituary when he died? By then I was features editor at the *Nashville Banner* newspaper. George Harrison came in for the funeral. His guitar gently wept at Carl's memorial service.

But my favorite time to see Cash was the one when we sneaked in the Ryman doors late at night, heard him close the joint down. And then we went back over to Tootsie's Orchid Lounge, just across the alleyway, for a beer. You didn't like beer. But you were there for the experience. I think Dad drank your beer. Or maybe I did.

Will the Circle Be Unbroken? I think it will be, Mom.

CHAPTER THIRTY

Kiss her goodbye

One other thing I'm glad of, Mom...if there is anything to be glad about at a time like this....is that Emily had her 6th birthday party at your house just the day before you had to come to the hospital.

I know you had hoped this summer you'd be able to get out of bed and get in the pool with the kids, but you never were able to. Still, on the day Emily had her party; Suzanne wheeled you to the big glass door that overlooks the pool. And you watched. You waved. You laughed at Joe as he did some of his silly things like falling flat-faced into the pool. You seemed so happy.

And so weak.

An hour or so later, we knew it was time to leave, so you could have peace and quiet. Emily went in to see you. "My precious Emily," you said. "I remember when I watched your Daddy change your stinky diapers."

You were talking about the old *Nashville Banner* days, when I worked at the afternoon newspaper and picked Emily up from daycare at about 3 in the afternoon. Most days, we'd go to your house for awhile.

You sure love that little girl.

You have a special bond with all your grandchildren.

Anyway, on that birthday, after Emily visited, Joey came in to see his "Nonny."

Then Suzanne led him out and I sat there as you smiled and gradually went off to sleep.

"Your mother's dying," Suzanne told me that night.

"She really is..." My wife cried and held me.

There was nothing to do but wait for that phone call.

And it came the next morning.

Still, the last thing, the last memory my children have of you is of the smiling, beautiful old woman who would tenderly stroke their heads.

You may have wanted them to come to the hospital, I don't know. And you couldn't really say.

All I know is I didn't want them to come down here now.

I want them to always have that memory of you laughing at the window, of you stroking their backs after they dried off and came in to kiss you goodbye.

Kiss you goodbye...

CHAPTER THIRTY-ONE

Remember when...?

My kids' memories of you will be warm, pure and peaceful. Kind of like the memories I have of my grandmothers.

Grandma Ghianni was feeding us ravioli and meatballs and Thanksgiving turkey the last time I saw her alive, before cancer claimed her.

Grandma Champ was enjoying Christmas at your house in Nashville the last time I saw her alive. We sang Christmas carols by the fireplace. It was that next year that leukemia got her.

I have mostly great, happy memories of my grandparents. Even Grandpa Ghianni. I didn't see him much, since he lived most of his decades in Long Beach, California. But I guess the strongest memory I have of him is of the day he took me for a long walk in Grand Rapids. He was visiting. We were looking for some ice cream.

But we stopped at fruit stands along the way. He'd buy an orange or a tomato; I can't remember what was in season. I just recall him feeling of the fruit and slicing it with his knife. I always wondered if that was the same knife he said he pulled on a cop who stopped him on his motorcycle in the early days of World War I. Can't remember why that occurred. Grandpa must have been in the right, because he got out of that alive.

Anyway, as we were wandering the streets of Grand Rapids, we even stopped in a bar for a drink. Or he did, anyway. I had ginger ale.

Then we had chocolate ice cream at a drug store soda fountain – "Timmy, you can have peanuts and a chocolate syrup if you want" – and walked back to our house at 507 Elliott Street where the profane old fellow poured himself another nip from his flask. I think Dad's still got that flask somewhere right next to the bottle of Jack Daniel's he was sharing with your dad, a shot a night, in the weeks before he died.

Mom, I know I've got to stop talking now.

And, well, it looks like your eyeballs aren't flickering as much, but I know you can still hear me.

There are still stories to tell; memories of a wonderful family.

Remember when Eric cut me over the lip with the saw when we were making a clubhouse in Grand Rapids?

Blood flowed everywhere. You held my head over the sink, as it filled with blood.

Dad almost passed out.

You got me to the hospital and I had stitches.

Remember when you woke Eric and me when we lived in Grand Rapids? The house was filled with smoke. Our furnace had begun to burn internally or something like that.

You called the fire department and we went next door to the Welmers' house. We watched out the window as the firemen first stopped the fire and then aired out the house. And you even let us stay home from school the next day, because we had been up most of the night.

Excitement on Elliott Street.

Speaking of the Welmers, you remember that the dad, Cal, had a used car lot at the edge of town just off the Beltway. He always was on the lookout for good deals for Dad. And he also would bring home sports cars when he had them in stock. I remember he'd take me for drives in most of them. A Morgan. MG. The '56 T-Bird. The original Corvette. It was that fascination with these fine machines that convinced me one day I would have a fine vehicle.

CHAPTER THIRTY-TWO

Some things I wanted to say

And it turned out that when I finally saved up enough to get a fancy car; you needed a new car too. You wanted something nice and sporty. We shopped on my days off. And on the same day, back in 1985, we ordered our Saabs.

Mine was a beautiful silver beast with rose interior. Yours white with blue interior.

My engine blew after maybe 150,000 hard miles.

Maybe someday I can talk Dad into letting me take your car off his hands.

You haven't been able to drive much in quite a while. But Dad still drives your car occasionally, just to keep it going. What have you got on it now after almost 15 years? 20,000 miles?

You sure looked great behind the wheel when you were strong enough to drive it.

The preacher's here now.

He wants to pray.

I've been talking to him a lot.

He says you want me to join the church and get the children baptized. He says it would be a great thing for me to do. Course, you know me. I'm gonna do it when I think it's good for the kids.

I suppose the Padre's right. But, well, you know me and preachers. I told him I'd get the kids baptized when I was good and ready.

He laughed at me.

I see you smiling a little now. Preacher's over in the corner now, listening to this. He's smirking, too. I guess I'm okay.

Anyway, Mom, I'll get around to it someday, I guess.

I still have problems with a God who would make you so sick, but even you told me that's just part of the deal. Play the hands you're dealt.

Preacher is leaving the room now.

I think you have to go back to sleep. Maybe not, though. Anyway, I guess I need to get some sleep. I'm gonna try to drive home in the morning to have breakfast with Suzanne and the kids.

The kids, the wife, that I wouldn't have if you hadn't stuck by me, given me strength.

Mom, everyone's left the room now.

I'm going to go in a minute.

I think they want to do your therapy and let you sleep for a while. Did you know that the doctors and nurses and all kinds of people came in here while I was talking?

Some of what I said may have been a little personal, I guess. Maybe they got uncomfortable, because a lot of them left.

Most of them probably still have their mothers.

And mine is going to die.

There were just some things I wanted to say.

They are telling me to leave the room for a while. Time for therapy.

Mom, I don't know if you can still hear me or not.

The monitors don't tell me much.

You are awfully still.

I'll go outside and grab a smoke and get some coffee. I'll come back and tell you more if you have time. If you don't decide to go somewhere.

I love you.

And, Mom, it's okay to stop fighting now.

CHAPTER THIRTY-THREE

No more

It was probably an hour later that I came back to her room. That time, I kissed her on the forehead and stroked her hand. There no longer were any signs that she was conscious.

In fact, there never were any signs like that again.

Chapter Thirty-Four

A spot on the ceiling

Well, true to my word, I gave the Padre his chance.

After he conducted the funeral for Mom, Suzanne and I began escorting Dad to church on Sundays.

Dad's sister, Aunt Rita, whom I love dearly, had come down for the funeral and stuck around quite awhile, to help Dad take care of the thank you notes and other necessities of getting through the grieving process.

"Son, we'd like you to visit, but we'd love you to stay awhile," said the Padre. "Actually, we'd like you to stay for good."

We did go. And we did stay. I found a spot on the ceiling that I focused on often during the service. It was my spot where I connected with my mom.

On the day after Christmas, Suzanne and I joined the church. The kids were baptized the following Sunday.

I wish Mom had been there.

Oh yeah, she was.

I keep forgetting.

After the baptisms, I looked up at the ceiling, at Mom's spot, and I winked.

The organ chimes sounded at the end of the service and I thought about that old line about what happens every time a bell rings.

And after church, after a baptism party at our house, I climbed into my little car, the one that spent so many nights parked outside the hospital just months before, and drove to the cemetery.

I wanted to tell Mom about the baptisms. Where do I start, I wondered, as I stood over her grave.

"Hi Mom, it's Tim."

CHAPTER THIRTY-FIVE

See you later

At first I went by the grave frequently, sat there on the bench that Dad had installed next to the monument.

He's got his spot reserved next to you. But, of course, none of us are in a hurry for him to join you.

Now, I don't come to the cemetery as often. Sometimes if I'm driving through the part of town where the cemetery dominates the landscape, I'll pull in and stop by to visit. Sometimes I just sit in my car and look up the hill at your monument. Other times I'll come up and sit down.

Suzanne put spring flowers on your grave the other day. I stopped to see them, to talk to you.

Figure I don't need to tell you much about what's happened since you saw the light.

I'm driving your white Saab, the one you bought when I bought the old silver one. Dad gave it to me about 10 years ago, after leaving it parked in the garage for quite awhile after you died.

It needed a lot of work to get it back into driving shape. It just passed 85,000 miles the other day, that's about 60,000 more than you put on it in 15 years. It runs pretty well. Needs a little cosmetic work on it.

My kids always joke me about a couple of things, one

being the automatic garage door opener of yours is still on the driver's side sun visor, just where you kept it. It doesn't open any doors any more. But I can't part with it. I'm a junk collector. And a sentimental guy.

I've got to wax the car soon. My friends think it's silly of me to drive this 28-year-old classic. I really don't make enough money to have any choice. No backup cars stashed anywhere.

But I really wouldn't have it any other way.

There even are those clear plastic oxygen tubes in the glove box. You kept them there in case of emergency. I just keep them, period.

I hope I can drive this car for a long time. I know, like you always told me, it's just a car. Material stuff can be replaced. But as long as I can drive it, I will.

You can see I'm not smoking now. I quit about a year after you died. My kids both had been bothering me about smoking. "When you gonna quit, Daddy? You're gonna die, Daddy. Stop using those fire sticks. We don't want you to die, Daddy."

Words are hard to hear sometime.

Finally, I kind of had to. Had a tumor on my neck. Wasn't cancer. But since they took such a big chunk, the doctor said the only way it would heal would be for me to stop smoking for six weeks. I was tempted to take it up again as soon as the six weeks was over. But I promised Suzanne and the kids I'd stop ... or at least take my best shot at it.

I've not smoked again. Sometimes I still miss it. Wish scientists would discover that smoking's good for you ....

I think I'm pretty much over most of my nasty habits. I have kept a close watch on my alcohol consumption. Occasional glass of wine or a beer at a ballgame. That's about it.

Sometimes I feel kind of odd, a fish out of water sort of thing, because my old friends all drink. I beg off. "Can't do you no harm to feel your own pain," my old pal, John Lennon, once sang when he was fighting his own demons of dope, cocaine, alcohol.

Sure wouldn't mind getting the giggles again sometime, uproarious laughter of friends drinking. But I don't do it. It's not the first glass that is the problem, of course. Nor the last. It's the ones in between that catch up to a guy.

There are so many times I wish I could see you again, sit and talk to you. I know you aren't really here at the cemetery beneath these six feet of dirt.

I know when I see you again it will be in heaven.

I've got too many things I could talk to you about.

We have a war or two going on right now. We usually do, I guess.

And I'm sure you know about the World Trade Center and September 11, 2001. Been at war ever since, in Afghanistan and Iraq. The one in Iraq never made sense to me. But it's more or less over. I hope.

Grandma would be happy that we have a black president, Barack Obama. I'm a pretty strong supporter. Dad isn't, of course. Not because Obama's black, but because he's a Democrat.

My old dog, Buddy, died about seven years ago. He had some sort of cancer or disease that couldn't be stopped. I still miss Buddy but am sure glad Suzanne stopped to help that "pot-bellied pig" that was in the road all those years ago.

Our pink cat, Pal, Buddy's best friend, the kitten I rescued from the bigger cats, is gone too. I guess about three years now.

But we couldn't stay without pets forever. Right around

the holidays of 2011-12, we decided to go get a dog and a cat. Began with the cat. Got him at the Humane Society. Picked him up on December 29, 2011. Your birthday. We named him Champ, for your maiden name, my middle name. A couple of years old, declawed and apparently very dizzy, as he has to stabilize himself by stretching out his front left leg. But he needed a home.

About a week later, we went to the dog pound and picked out a little German Shepherd-Siberian Husky mix. Named her Roxy. Like the theater in Clarksville where The News Brothers held their movie premiere.

I guess you know I saw the Rolling Stones a couple more times in concert. No foxes to interrupt the drive home. I know, it's only rock 'n' roll. But I still like it...just as much as I did when I'd play the jukebox in the old malt shop in Grand Rapids...as much as when I had that collection of 45s that you and Dad and your friends played on your 40th birthday.

I guess you know about the Great Nashville Flood of 2010 and how it destroyed half our house. But we got it back now. Even wrote a book about that, published it on the Internet. I'm sure you know about that now.

My buddy, Rob Dollar, and I even published a hardcover book about our adventures as newsmen, *When Newspapers Mattered: The News Brothers & their Shades of Glory.* People who have read it like it. Some are surprised by how much time I spent getting too close to the flame. You wouldn't be surprised. You aren't, I guess.

Emily's started reading some of your old mystery books. Started with Agatha Christie ones.

Joe, well, he doesn't read as much. He mostly likes to listen to music. He's not much into The Beatles or even

Johnny Cash or Elvis. Could care less that Kris Kristsofferson has become a good friend of mine.

Joe likes Tom Petty and The Stones okay.

But he's a Satchmo guy. He loves Louis Armstrong. Up until Hurricane Katrina a few years ago, we went to New Orleans every summer and took the kids to Preservation Hall. You know all about that storm, I guess. A few old jazz men joined the heavenly choir and band then, I'm sure.

I'm just rambling.

It's a warm day. The flowers are pretty.

Every time I come out here, I talk about different stuff. Sometimes I complain about work, about how newspapers are dying. I'm a freelancer now. Newspaper bought me and a bunch of us older guys out. There are a lot of things that don't make a whole lot of sense.

But one thing is for sure, I still need a haircut.

You know that. Fact is, when I got "bought out" at the newspaper, I decided I wasn't going to get a haircut any more. Everyone needs a hobby. Mine is growing my hair. Grew it out to where it stopped by itself, as the old song "Hair" goes.

How do you like the pony-tail?

Thunderstorm coming. I better get going. Windows are open on the old Saab down there at the bottom of the hill.

I'll be back soon, to talk about my life.

See you later, Mom.